CONTENTS

MAKE THE MOST OF YOUR GUIDE

Reading these two pages will help you to get the most out of your guide and save you time when using it. Sites discussed in the text are cross-referenced with the cover maps – for example, the reference 'Map D–C3' refers to the Vienna Map (Map D), column C, row 3. Use the Map Plan below to quickly locate the map you need.

MAP PLAN

Outside Back Cover   Outside Front Cover

Inside Front Cover   Inside Back Cover

THE BIGGER PICTURE

Key to Map Plan

A – Schönbrunn

B – Donaupark and Prater

C – Hofburg

D – Vienna

E – Excursions

F – Vienna Transport Map

4

The best of
VIENNA

PAUL TINGAY

NH
NEW
HOLLAND

GLOBETROTTER™

First edition published in 2008
by New Holland Publishers (UK) Ltd
London • Cape Town • Sydney • Auckland
10 9 8 7 6 5 4 3 2 1

website: www.newhollandpublishers.com

Garfield House, 86 Edgware Road
London W2 2EA
United Kingdom

80 McKenzie Street
Cape Town 8001
South Africa

Unit 1, 66 Gibbes Street
Chatswood, NSW 2067
Australia

218 Lake Road
Northcote, Auckland
New Zealand

Distributed in the USA by
The Globe Pequot Press, Connecticut

ISBN 978 1 84773 015 2

Publishing Manager: Thea Grobbelaar
DTP Cartographic Manager: Genené Hart
Editor: Nicky Steenkamp
Designer: Nicole Bannister

Cartographers: Genené Hart, Lauren Fick
Picture Researchers: Zainoenisa Manuel
Consultants: Mathias Kleemann, Carole French
Proofreader: Mariëlle Renssen

Reproduction by Resolution (Cape Town)
Printed and bound by Times Offset (M) Sdn. Bhd.,
Malaysia.

This guidebook has been written by independ-
ent authors and updaters. The information
therein represents their impartial opinion, and
neither they nor the publishers accept payment
in return for including in the book or writing
more favourable reviews of any of the establish-
ments. Whilst every effort has been made to
ensure that this guidebook is as accurate and up
to date as possible, please be aware that the
facts quoted are subject to change, particularly
the price of food, transport and accommoda-
tion. The Publisher accepts no responsibility or
liability for any loss, injury or inconvenience
incurred by readers or travellers using this guide.

Photographic Credits:
Caroline Jones: page 70; **David Bowden:**
front cover, pages 51, 61, 65; **Fresh Food
Images/Photo Access:** page 66;
Imagebroker/Photo Access: page 25;
Imagestate/Photo Access: page 33;
International PhotoBank: pages 6, 27, 28, 74;
Jon Smith: pages 13, 16, 17, 20, 34, 36, 41,
46, 47, 49, 71, 84; **Neil Setchfield:** page 52,
60, 76; **Paul Tingay:** pages 7, 10, 15, 21, 22,
23, 24, 29, 31, 32, 44, 50, 63, 75, 77, 78;
Photo Access: page 79; **Pictures Colour
Library:** pages 18, 42, 54, 72, 73, 82; **Robin
McKelvie:** page 53; **Sime/Photo Access:** title,
pages 19, 26, 45, 80; **Travel Pix
Collection/Jonarnoldimages.com:** page 30

Front Cover: A view of the entrance to Café
Central, a coffee house in Vienna.
Title Page: All of Vienna haggled over the
construction of the modern Haas Haus,
Stephansplatz.

Key to Symbols

⊠ — address   ⊕ — opening times

☎ — telephone   🚌 — transport

🕿 — fax   🔔 — entry fee

🖥 — website   🍽 — restaurants nearby

🖅 — e-mail address   🚇 — U-Bahn or S-Bahn station

Map Legend

motorway		motorway	
national road		main road	Tunnel
main road		road	
railway		mall	MALL
route number	96a E26	built-up area	
international boundary		building of interest	☐
country name	HUNGARY	post office	⊠
river and dam	Donau (Danube)	underground	U
peak	Obersberg ▲1467 m	rapid transit	S
city	☐ VIENNA	parking	P
major town	⊙ St Pölten	police station	•
town	○ Baden	hospital	⊕
large village	◎ Melk	bus terminus	🚍
village	○ Rust	library	📖
ruin	∴	one-way street	→
monastery	🛐	place of worship	△ Votivkirche
castle	♜	tourist information	ℹ
gate	↔		
hotel	Ⓗ SACHER	museum	■
place of interest	★ Theatre	university	■
airport	✈	college	■
restaurant	Ⓡ	school	■
park & garden	☐ ☐	market	■

Keep us Current

Travel information is apt to change, which is why we regularly update our guides. We'd be most grateful to receive feedback from you if you've noted something we should include in our updates. If you have any new information, please share it with us by writing to the Publishing Manager, Globetrotter, at the office nearest to you (addresses on the imprint page of this guide). The most significant contribution to each new edition will be rewarded with a free copy of the updated guide.

VIENNA

Across the street a music student plays a Mozart serenade, violin case for coins at her formal skirt. In the spring sunshine, the sidewalk café is already busy. A fresh rose on each table, waiters in white shirts, black ties. An open *fiaker* hackney trots past. A young mum pushes twins in their pram as a chimney sweep in traditional bellhop cap parks his Harley. Above the passers-by gleams the copper-green dome of St Michael, guardian gate into the Imperial Palace. There is the aroma of freshly ground coffee, cinnamon-hint strudel, crispy Kaiser-semmel rolls, Sachertorte with cream, the snap of newspapers, the buzz of conversation. Grüss Gott. Welcome to Vienna.

Jewish Culture

In 1896 Vienna was host to the world's first Jewish, or Jüdisches, Museum – closed by the Nazis in 1938. Today's museum in Dorotheergasse is a fascinating celebration of Viennese Jewish culture. Modern, eclectic, its three floors reveal a powerful portrait of the Jewish contribution to Vienna's artistic, political and medical history and the Jews' relationship down the centuries with a usually hostile Gentile populace. Writers Arthur Schnitzler and Josef Roth, composers Arnold Schönberg and Johann Strauss, and psychoanalyst Sigmund Freud were all Jewish.

The Land

Waltz maestro Johann Strauss's Schönen Blauen Donau (Beautiful Blue Danube) rises in Germany's Black Forest and, like the dance, the river twists and twirls ever faster as it flows east through country after country to the Black Sea 2859km (1776 miles) away.

Vienna is the **capital of Austria**, in central Europe. The country covers an area of 83,855km^2 (32,368 sq miles), roughly the size of Scotland. Although much of it is winelands, fruit farms, forest and skiing alps, 70% of the Austrian population are city dwellers. The city spreads in a horseshoe shape back from the **Danube** and its fringing slopes of grapevines to the **Wienerwald**, the Vienna Woods, inspiration to music maestros Beethoven, Mozart and Schubert. The Danube to the east has been artificially divided into four rivers to prevent flooding. The historic and once-walled centre of Vienna is a walking city. If you are map-wise and don't pause too long to admire the awesome plethora of museums, churches, squares and old-world cafés, you can stroll its 2km (1.6 miles) north to south, or east to west, in under three hours. But you won't. There is simply too much to see: the ethereal clouds, cupids, saints and nymphs in Baroque churches, the prancing white horses of the Spanish Riding School, the Vienna Boys' Choir (there are four choirs incidentally), *fiaker* hackney cabs and twisty cobbled alleyways.

Vienna's ancient inner city has seen the **Roman** legions come and go, provided a home to practically every musical genius in the western world and by dint of war, diplomacy and above all astute marriage manoeuvring, allowed one family, the **Habsburg** dynasty (15th–20th century), to rule half of Europe for 640 years.

The **Wienerwald** is a great arc of forested hills and meadows on the edge of the city's suburbs. It stretches from the Danube Valley in the north to the foothills of the Austrian Alps in the south. It is a huge, hilly, untouched and heavily forested area of 1250km^2 (483 sq miles) with hide-away cycling tracks and tiny villages. It has always

> **Meet the Volk**
> Viennese are no more German than the Irish are English. One in three Viennese buys a newspaper and every-one loves lying on the sunny green banks of the Danube. The Viennese, even in a traffic accident, are soft-spoken; there's no feeling of big-city aggression and every-one is honest to a fault. Folk on the U-Bahn are better at pretending not to look at you than in other European cities. Menial jobs are mainly done by immigrants from Eastern Europe.

Opposite: *A treble clef of flowers points to Mozart's statue.*
Below: *City view of Northern Vienna's district.*

been the Viennese R'n'R area with families sometimes spending all summer in the bracing wilderness. There are 40 mountain-biking trails, always a little restaurant around the next corner, view points, small lakes, rivers, toboggan runs and even a few humble skiing slopes.

History in Brief

In AD433 Vienna, known as **Vindobona**, was an outpost of Roman Carnuntum, Province of Pannonia Superior, and under attack by relentless Mongols, Goths, Huns and Vandals.

Although it was the opportunist **Ottokar II** of Bohemia who started building the **Hofburg** (*see* page 45), initially a rough fort, it was the **Habsburgs** who turned Vienna into what it is today. The remote castle of Habichtsberg overlooking the River Reuss in today's Switzerland was the Habsburg's ancestral *schloss*. **Rudolf of Habsburg**, the German king, killed Ottokar in battle. His family then ruled Austria, from Vienna, for the next 640 years until Austria was defeated in **World War I**. The family also held on to the title of Holy Roman Emperor from 1440 until forced by Napoleon to abandon it in 1806.

Politics, money and the delights of the flesh have occupied the Viennese as much as any people. But in Vienna, religious argument always seemed more important. Soon after revolutionary reformer **Martin Luther** dramatically arrived on the scene, nationalism, politics, economics, social justice, religious schism and war became inextricably entwined.

Every ceiling, cupola, corner, wall and interior surface packed with marble columns, gilt twirls,

Below: *Austria's red and white flag flutters on every tram.*

pastel saints, cherubs, puff pastry clouds in a phantasmagoria of ornamentation is one way of describing the **Baroque** style which took Vienna's rich and religious by storm in the 17th and 18th centuries. The word Baroque comes from that for the rough or imperfectly shaped pearl, and covers a flourishing mixture of classical architecture, drama, literature, music and the visual arts. The colours are gorgeous, the gilt awesome and the attention to detail staggering; it is rather like repeatedly walking into a series of Aladdin caves in its freedom of form, motion and feeling. The absolute monarchs of Europe, including the Habsburgs, adored it and tried very hard to convert every church and palace into the new style.

The age of Copernicus, calculus, printing press and new world discovery arrived. Better agricultural techniques prompted an agricultural revolution but also migration to the cities and the start of industrialization. In the German-speaking lands of the Empire, Goethe's blood and thunder had to compete with recently invented pop novels.

World War I

Rampant nationalism led to World War I. It was sparked by the assassination of **Archduke Franz Ferdinand**, heir to the Habsburg throne.

Millions died in the war, food was scarce, the empire was defeated, the coffee-house culture collapsed, and Vienna's first **socialist mayor** turned the postwar city into 'Red Vienna', with the construction of huge housing estates and major reforms in welfare, education and care for the workers. But this display of Marxist socialism created

Diplomatic Affairs
Three kings, two emperors, 11 princes, 90 ambassadors and a host of hangers-on met under the chairmanship of Prince Metternich of Austria at the Congress of Vienna in 1814–15, a nine-month summit and the world's first, to decide who should have what chunk of territory after Napoleon's 25 years of revolutionary warfare. It wasn't all decorous diplomacy. Wilhemina, Duchess of Sagan, and Princess Catherine Bagration ('the naked angel') soon came to be known as *les grandes horizontales*, the Tsar being particularly susceptible to their charms. There were cheese competitions, sleighing forays in the Vienna Woods, tournaments, ballooning and firework displays. Beethoven premiered and conducted his *Fidelio*, 6000 guests came to one ball, and the waltz became the most popular dance in Europe.

Above*: Adolf Hitler addresses the people of Vienna in 1938, at Heldenplatz, Hofburg.*

tension and led to the rise of the **Nazis**.

Although most Austrians wanted to link up with Germany at the end of World War I, by 1938 they sought their own independence. To pre-empt a referendum on the issue, Austrian-born Adolf Hitler marched into Austria and fabricated a plebiscite in favour of **Anschluss**, or unification, whereupon 42 synagogues were razed and the killings began. Some 250,000 Austrians were conscripted into the German World War II military, and nearly all died. It was worse for the Jewish community. Many had escaped, but 65,000 were slaughtered in the death camps. About 100,000 Austrians were imprisoned in Germany or in concentration camps, and 10,000 died in Gestapo custody. The Nazis in Austria did not have it all their own way, however, especially from 1944 onwards. **Resistance fighters**, code-named **05**, fought long and hard. About 2700 Jews were executed by the Nazis.

Vienna was bombed by the RAF and Allied forces on 52 occasions. The State Opera, Albertina Art Gallery, the Tiergarten in the Schönbrunn Palace gardens, all the city's bridges and 87,000 houses were hit; 24,000 Viennese lost their lives. Worse was the so-called 'liberation' of Vienna by the **Soviet army**. Encouraged by their officers, the troops raped some 90,000 Viennese women, and stole or removed practically everything in the city.

Government and Economy

Half the population owns computers and every second person a car (Jaguars are popular). The average income is in excess of US$36,000 per annum, just below Japan. There was a 389% increase in value of trade from 2000–2005. Austria's **exports** are valued at US$112 billion with a trade balance at US$3 billion. Its principal exports are machinery, motor vehicles, paper products, steel, textiles and foodstuffs, accounting for US$45 billion per annum. But it is in **high-tech services** (banking, finance, consulting, engineering) that it scores. Austria is one of the world's top 10 **tourist** destinations, earning the country US$15.6 billion.

Austrian **agriculture** only accounts for 2.2% of GDP: wine, potatoes, grains, dairy products, fruit, cattle and pigs. The country's natural resources include oil, coal, iron ore, copper, zinc, lignite and hydropower. About 85% of the country is rural and, of that, 17% is agricultural land.

The countryside, or *Länder*, usually votes conservative Catholic while Vienna is socialist. Austria flirted with Nazi fascism 70 years ago, which occasionally comes back to haunt it. Head of state is the directly elected Federal President, head of government the Chancellor. Every municipality has a powerful mayor. Parliament and Vienna's town hall, or Rathaus, are on the Ringstrasse. Austrian politics tend to swing left and right, making everyone uneasy. A former President and UN Secretary-General, **Kurt Waldheim** took a hammering abroad if not in Austria on his war record, and one **Jörg Haider**, a former leader of the Austrian Freedom Party, occasionally rears his strident voice.

The Spy that Loved Him

It was 05:55 on 24 May 1913 when one Nizetas collected a letter from the main post office in Vienna. It was a letter with instructions and money from the Russian secret service. The Austrian Spooks knew it and had set a trap. Nizetas was in fact Alfred Redi, colonel and head of the Imperial Austrian army's counter espionage service. He was homosexual and had been blackmailed. Chased through the Innere Stadt, he was caught, handed a pistol and told to do what officers and gentlemen did. He shot himself. All very discreet. But journalist Egon Kisch broke the juicy homosexuality and espionage bits and became a tabloid hero. Redi's lover later married, had children and lived happily ever after.

The People

There was a time in Vienna when you could not be received at the imperial court if you were 'not born'. Of the nobility, that is. Revolutions, wars and cheeky democracy put paid to that.

There are 8.1 million Austrians – roughly the number of Londoners – of whom 1.6 million live in Vienna. Some 15% are under 15 and 28% over 60. Adult literacy stands at 99% and women tend to have on average 1.4 babies (so to speak). Some Viennese are **immigrants**, mainly from the former and neighbouring Soviet satellites and others from the Balkans and heavily populated Nigeria. Polite Pakistanis and Indians seem to monopolize newspaper stands. The favourite names for girl babies, by far, are Leonie and Lena. And for boys, Tobias is the most popular, with Elias a losing second. Males in Austria are called up for national service. To be called 'Doktor' or 'Professor' in Vienna is apparently enormously comforting. About 58% of Vienna's tourists are from Germany.

To an outsider, the Viennese can initially seem reserved. Head waiters in the grand cafés sometimes try their old-fashioned aloofness on newcomers. It's a historical act that goes with the sumptuous *bellestriste* décor and can quite easily be ameliorated.

Men wear cashmere suits in the inner city; young women wear jeans and boots. Fast-food outlets, especially *wurst* (sausage) stands, are popular with the commuters. Bicycle riding and walking are regular pastimes. There are bicycle paths fringing the busy streets; pedestrians give way to them. Theatre, western classical music and

opera are favourites. Above all, Vienna is a **pavement café society**.

Transport is excellent, the tap water perfect, scientific research is on the increase, and there are some very noisy motorways along the Gürtel. Vienna is one of the safest cities in the world.

Speak a few words from your German phrase book, and you will be greeted with a smile, a torrent of German and then fluent English, Vienna's second language.

The Viennese speak **German**, but it takes a German to distinguish the Viennese way of speaking. One tram ride watching the shops will throw up a host of English street advertising. The Viennese have many words and expressions all their own. They include some that are incomprehensible to other German speakers such as *Beisl*: tavern; *Stiftl*: wine glass; *Grüss Gott*: hello; *Hasse*: sausage.

Signs on underground escalators will advise you to *bitte rechts stehen* (please stand on the right). The University of Vienna (there are 13 universities in Vienna) offers inexpensive 9–12-week courses in German and there are several private institutions (e.g. Berlitz).

Above: *The Volksgarten, one of Vienna's many green parks, is much loved by children.*

✿ *See* Map D–E2   ★★★

STEPHANSDOM

There are 660 Catholic churches in Vienna. Head, shoulders, surrounding platz and soaring spire above the many Catholic churches in Vienna rises the great Stephansdom (**St Stephen's Cathedral**), with its 137m (450ft) *steffl*, or steeple, which visitors in good wind can reach by climbing up the stairway. The cornerstone, of today's church was laid in 1137, although much of the cathedral was built in the 14th century to its present Gothic style. Its interior was given a Baroque makeover during the 17th century. In 1711, the 'Pummerin,' an immense bell, was cast from captured Turkish cannons and placed in the North, or pagan, tower (the church has four towers). By 1732 the bells called the faithful to an average of 150 masses celebrated in the cathedral per day.

Stephansdom saw the Turkish wars, hand-to-hand fighting in the 1809 Napoleonic conflict, and half of it was destroyed by fire following Russian artillery attacks that hit surrounding houses in 1945.

The roof of the cathedral is 110m (361ft) long and is so pitched that the rain's drain-off power cleans it. It consists of 605 tons of steel – replacing a veritable forest of 3000 Gothic tree trunks – and 230,000 glazed and zigzag roof tiles, each of which weighs 2.5kg (5.5lb).

When the sun pours through Stephansdom's vast array of needle windows, the dappled light fragments the interior into a treasure chest. It lights up the patterned floor of the central nave, the huge fluted columns, each filigree pillar decorated by a life-size saint (107 of them), dozens of

Opposite: *One of the many altars in St Stephen's Cathedral.*

painting-backed altars, stained glass, unbelievably soaring vaulting and much gilt. Carvings of the Madonna include the 1320 one, called *Madonna of the Domestics*, where early-to-work servant girls heard Mass. As composer Frédéric Chopin wrote (Christmas 1830): 'It is an immense space in which silence reigns.'

On one interior wall of the North tower, which was never finished and subsequently topped with a Baroque cupola, there is a **statue of Jesus** called the 'Christ with a Toothache.' At one time it was mounted on the outside of the church, and drunken night-time passers-by would mock Jesus' agonized face, asking if he had a toothache, whereupon they were all afflicted by toothache themselves and only cured when they begged forgiveness of the statue.

The working draft plans of the cathedral, the world's largest Gothic collection, are kept in Vienna's **Historical Museum** in Karlsplatz.

As in the old medieval city, all roads (mud tracks at the time) lead, star-like, to the **cathedral** and its busy and huge cobbled **square**. Like in medieval times, there are nearby food stands, hackney cabs by the north wall, hawkers of Mozart concerts in 18th-century costume, leaflet distributors, ice-cream vendors, flower sellers, tour groups, genuine pilgrims and a rolling half-an-hour-each repertory of musicians, dancers and buskers entertaining the ever-moving crowds.

Domes and Spires
Ruprechtskirche, built originally in the 8th century, is Romanesque – Vienna's oldest but with modern stained-glass windows. Today's Stephansdom (on the site of a 12th-century church) is the great Gothic cathedral in the centre of the city. Karlskirche's green Baroque dome and Trajan columns were built in 1737. Michaels-kirche has a medieval 13th-century interior and Baroque high altar. Jesuitenkirche (1623–31) has marble column after marble column.

☆ *See* Map D–D2   ★★★

Above*: Palais Ferstel, built by Heinrich Ferstel between 1856 and 1860.*
Opposite*: Judenplatz Holocaust Memorial. Each stone, a book, a life lost.*

SCHOTTENSTIFT

The monastery of Schottenstift, dating back 850 years, was named after Scottish (but actually Irish) monks. Only a few corners remain of its ancient Romanesque interior; it's now 18th-century Baroque – lush marble columns, gold flourishes, pastel ceiling paintings and doleful pictures of heaven-hallucinating saints. The highlight in the museum is a multi-panelled hinged **altarpiece**, featuring Joseph and Mary's biblical flight with the baby Jesus from King Herod to safety in Egypt 2000 years ago. Rather charmingly, medieval Vienna forms the backdrop.

FREYUNG MARKET

The name of the 'Freyung' facing the monastery church and museum means 'sanctuary'. In an age of banditry and uncertainty, monasteries were often fortified refuges around which farming and villages developed. It is an oblong, cobbled square flanked by the 1946 nymph-decorated Austria fountain. Freyung hums with action. There are two **pavement cafés** with snappy service, one specializing in exotic ice-cream sundaes. The ad hoc **stalls** in the **market** sell organic products (the largest selection in Austria, they say), toys,

☆ *See* Map D–D2   ★★★

baskets, home-made jams, jewellery, fruit schnapps (corn schnapps is more a German speciality), with parties of ladies enjoying a glass of wine at the collapsible tables.

Freyung, in the days before football fever and pop concerts, was quite the entertainment centre as it was here that public executions were held. Here, too, is the **Schubladenkastenhaus**, or Chest of Drawers house, built in 1774. The **Café Central** is round the corner. It has vaulted ceilings, smart-jacketed waiters, newspapers from all over the world and elegant coffees, and was the intelligentsia's favourite 100 years ago.

HOLOCAUST MEMORIAL

A quiet lane leads from Am Hof to a cobbled square surrounded by gracious buildings. In the middle of this square stands a silent stone block the height of two men. The **Judenplatz Jewish Holocaust Memorial** was designed by British sculptor, Rachel Whiteread. It has no colour, no ornamentation, just two closed doors, a raised plinth and row after row of chiselled

books, each frozen page commemorating the loss of the 65,000 Austrian men, women and children that were slaughtered by the Nazis during the Holocaust, simply because they happened to be Jews.

To Market, to Market
You will inevitably come across a midweek or Saturday market. There is the Friday and Saturday Organic Market in Freyung in the Innere Stadt, and the flea market, or *Flohmarkt*, on Saturdays at Kettenbrückengasse 5. The Brunnenmarkt at 16 Brunnengasse stretches for a kilometre and is open Monday–Saturday. The Art and Crafts *Kunstmarkt* is held in a monastic courtyard at 1 Heiligenkreuzerhof from April to September, but only on the first weekend of the month. The largest of them all is the Naschmarkt, a Vienna phenomenon of fruit, vegetables, spices and restaurants. From mid-November onwards there are 'child Jesus', or *Christkindlmärkte*, at the Rathaus, Karlsplatz, Schönbrunn and Spittelberg, with much joviality and *glühwein*.

See Map C–D1

★★★

SPANISH RIDING SCHOOL

You will often hear a student opera singer or musician playing in the lofty portals of St Michael's Gate. The shop inside will tell you about the **Lipizzaner horses** of the Spanish Riding School and the museum. The stalls for 65 of the highly trained white horses are just behind St Michael's Church, on the corner of Habsburgergasse and Reitschulgasse. Go through the arch in the latter and you will come to the **equestrian monument** to Kaiser Josef II on Josefsplatz. It was erected in 1541 by Gerardus Mercator, the Latinized name of the Flemish cartographer Gerhard Kremer (1512–94), the inventor of the revolutionary Mercator map projection.

Art on Horseback

Ghengis Khan, Alexander the Great, the US 6th cavalry and the derby would have been impossible if man had not tamed the horse and brought horses to Europe from Central Asia 3500 years ago. The horses of the Spanish Riding School, Lipizzaners, have been bred since 1580. They are white horses but when born can be black. It takes about eight years to train a rider. The most spectacular of the horses' highly trained leaps are the *Levade, Courbette* and above all the Capriole where the horse leaps and kicks out its hind legs. The riders wear cocked hats, 19th-century military-style uniform and do not use stirrups. The Spanish Riding School performances are actually held inside the Winter Riding School, a 55m (180ft) long, chandelier-decorated hall of the Hofburg Palace.

See Map C–E2 | ★★★

Left: *Inside the National Library, you will find a collection of over 7.4 million items. A very extensive list includes manuscripts, rare books that are very old, maps, globes, portraits, music and posters.*
Opposite: *All the beauty of the Lipizzaner horse is seen in motion: its grace lies in the harmony of movements.*

PRUNKSAAL AND NATIONAL LIBRARY

The magnificent Prunksaal, or **State Hall** and **National Library**, is architect Johann Bernhard Fischer von Erlach's masterpiece (he also designed the Schönbrunn Palace and Karlskirche). The Baroque interior of the Prunksaal is all marble pillars, ceiling frescos, statues, twirling staircases, balconies, and wooden gilded bookcases. It safeguards approximately 200,000 leather-bound books, including a 15th-century Gutenberg Bible. Johannes Gutenberg (1398–1468) invented modern book printing, although the earliest known printed book, the *Diamond Sutra* (10th century), is in India. The huge library is 78m (85yd) long and two storeys high and has some 2.5 million books. Long ladders help staff access the books. The courtyard of the Prunksaal is where black marketeer Harry Lime wanted the military authorities to believe he was run down by a truck in the 1949 film *The Third Man*.

National Library
⊠ 1, Josefsplatz,
🚇 Karlsplatz/Oper
U1, U3: Stephansplatz
U3: Herrengasse
☎ 534 10-0
🖥 www.onb.ac.at
✉ onb@onb.ac.at
🕓 Tue–Sun
10:00–18:00,
Thu 10:00–21:00,
closed Mondays.
💰 Admission costs for exhibitions.

Spanish Riding School
⊠ Michaelerplatz 1,
A–1010 Wien
☎ (43) 1 533 9031
🖥 www.srs.at
🕓 Tue–Sat
09:00–16:00,
Fri 09:00–19:00,
closed Mondays.

☆ *See* Map D–C3/C4   ★★★

MUSEUMS QUARTIER

The new Museums Quartier (or MQ) complex across the Burgring motorway is one of the world's largest centres of culture and the arts. It includes an **Architectural Museum**, **Museum of Modern Art** (MUMOK), the dance training centre of the **Tanzquartier Wien**, the **ZOOM** children's museum, the **Arts Hall**, math space and the **Leopold Museum** of Austrian art with more than 5000 works. The MQ complex sprawls in an elegant modern architectural weave over a huge area. In the Leopold Museum, there is the world's largest collection of Austrian artist Egon Schiele's works. He died at the age of 28.

The main courtyard, **Quartier 21**, of the Museums Quartier is becoming the cool locality to hang out: bars, restaurant, art book-shop, ice-cream vendors, music and students draped on every ledge, plus studios for young avant garde artists, and record shops and designer clothes boutiques. Much of the Museums Quartier is open 24 hours a day and the bars and cafés well into the early morning. The **Tobacco Museum** contains 2500

Museums Quartier
✉ Museumsplatz 1, 1070 Wien
🖥 www.mqw.at

Architekturzentrum Wien:
🕐 10:00–19:00.
🖥 www.azw.at
Kunsthalle Wien:
🕐 open daily 10:00–19:00, Thu 10:00–22:00.
🖥 www. kunsthallewien.at
Leopold Museum:
🕐 open daily 10:00–18:00, Thu 10:00–21:00.
🖥 www.leopold museum.org
MUMOK:
🕐 open daily 10:00–18:00, Thu 10:00–21:00.
🖥 www.mumok.at
Tansquartier Wien:
🖥 www.tqw.at
Quartier 21:
🕐 open daily 10:00–20:00, except special events.
🖥 www.quartier21. mqw.at
ZOOM Kinder-museum:
🕐 Mon–Fri 08:30–17:00, Sat–Sun and school holidays 10:00–17:30.
🖥 www.kinder museum.at

MUSEUMS QUARTIER

exhibits. Tobacco was introduced to the West 500 years ago by Spanish and Portuguese seamen returning from the Caribbean.

The **Kunsthistorisches Museum** is an exact Italian neo-Renaissance twin of the **Natural History Museum** opposite. It houses the world's largest collection of Dutch artist **Pieter Breughel**'s (1525–69) art. Apparently he used to dress up in peasant clothes to be able to mingle among the poor country folk and paint his evocative canvases of their lifestyle.

There are galleries of **Rembrandt van Rijn** (1606–69), a huge collection of **Peter Paul Rubens** (1577–1640), **Jan Vermeer**, British artist **Thomas Gainsborough**, **Hans Holbein**, **Joshua Reynolds**, **Titian** (1488–1576), **Veronese**, **Tintoretto**, **Raphael** (1483–1520), **Caravaggio** (1571–1610), **Velázquez, van Dyck** and an excellent German collection, the so-named 'Danube School', including **Albrecht Dürer** (1471–1528).

The museum with its 8000 works (the world's fourth largest art collection), of which only 800 are on display, is a gargantuan feast.

> **Museums**
> There are some 80 museums and galleries in Vienna: Baroque and Medieval Art, Military museum, Applied Arts, National History, Church museums, Music museums, a Map museum, Children's museum, and in fact a whole Museums Quartier. The treasures of the Habsburg Emperors in Hofburg Palace include the Royal China and Silverware, historical weaponry and fascinating, if at times macabre, works of religious art.

Left: *The Kunsthistorisches Museum (gallery of art), faces the Natural History Museum.*
Opposite: *The buildings of the Museums Quartier are a mix of old and stylishly new.*

☆ See Map D–D4 | ★★★

THE SECESSION BUILDING

The 1898 Secession Art Gallery, named after Vienna's modern, or Jugendstil, art movement and nicknamed Golden Cabbage Head, has a dome, or rather a bees nest, of golden laurel leaves. Beneath it are the words: 'To each its art, to art its freedom.' And you have to be pretty arty to appreciate the symbolism of Gustav Klimt's frieze of Beethoven inside. Based on his 9th Symphony, its nude figure of Beethoven and bare walls got a pretty frigid reception when it was first displayed in 1902. Outside is a bronze (clothed) statue of Shakespeare's **Mark Antony**, replete and obese in his chariot pulled by a pride of (presumably Cleopatra's) desert lions. The **Secessionists** broke away from the mainstream **Austrian Artist's Association** in 1897 to form their own coterie, free of the copycat historicism that, for example, dominates the buildings of the Ringstrasse.

Opposite: *Dates and sweetmeats, fruit and fish to shatter any diet at the bohemian Naschmarkt.*
Right: *Tantalizing cuisine aromas waft up from the nearby Naschmarkt to the Golden Cabbage Head atop the Secession Art Gallery.*

See Map D–D4 | ★★

NASCHMARKT

There are midweek and Saturday food markets all over Vienna's suburbs but the biggest and the busiest is the **Naschmarkt** just off Karlsplatz. Its long avenue of stalls and

eateries is packed with folk hunting fruit, spices, fish, cheese and 'deli' offerings.

In this harlequin village you can choose from 100 varieties of cheese, a Pandora's display of Persian spices, Slav nibbles, Viennese wines, Chinese takeaways, Turkish fish and a mesmerizing array of goodies. It is also a **Saturday flea market** of Indian silks, T-shirts, leather goods, jewellery, furs, dubious Russian icons, porcelain, tin toys, antique watches, and 'Roman' coins. You will see every nationality, hear every language. Come Christmas Eve, a light snow falling, everyone is your friend as the mulled wine mellows into *Gemütlichkeit*.

STADTPARK

You can still walk along the old **River Wien** as it cuts through Vienna's **Stadtpark** off Parkring. Largest of the green lungs that surround the Inner City, the park's main claim to fame is the 1925 **Strauss monument**. Depicting the larger-than-life waltz king, violin in hand and gilded from head to toe, it is framed by an arch of naked river nymphs playing musical chairs.

A Loaf of Bread, a Glass of Wine

Wines in Vienna include the Grüner Veltliner with its fruity bouquet, often with a hint of pepper. Most of the wine grown in and around Vienna is of this grape variety. Rieslings are traditionally produced in Wachau along the Danube. The Roter Zweigelt with its full aromatic bouquet is Austria's most popular red wine, while the Blaufränkisch is fruity and slightly sour. The Blauer Portugieser has a touch of violets and contains little alcohol. *Most* (must), the juice of freshly pressed grapes, and *Sturm*, which is neither must nor wine, but a stage of fermentation between the two, are also very popular. When fermentation comes to an end, the unfiltered young wine is called Staubiger, or 'dusty one'. A Heuriger is a wine tavern as well as a wine made from the latest crop.

☆ *See* Map D–A5 | ★★

HITLER'S APARTMENT

Possibly the most intriguing address off shop-to-drop Mariahilferstrasse is No. 28 Stumpergasse. It was here that young **Adolf Hitler** lived when he first came to Vienna in 1907.

'Never forget' – *Niemals Vergessen* – reads today's chunky memorial slab from Mauthausen Concentration Camp outside the former Métropole Hotel (now Leopold-Figl-Hof) in Morzinplatz, former **Gestapo HQ**.

Not Hitler's apartment, his favourite Café Sperl, or the Neue Burg Balcony at Heldenplatz where he announced the Anschluss, or the grand Hotel Impérial where he stayed that fateful night, have any indication that he was there. There are no furled flags like every other historic building, no plaques, no mention in tourist literature. Even when the sins of the fathers are *not* those of the sons, it appears the pain of a generation past haunts Vienna still.

THIRD MAN MUSEUM

Vienna was in ruins, rubble on every street, and Stephansdom all but razed to the ground. Electricity was intermittent, water pipes had burst, there were long queues for bread. The hospitals were barely working and no-one trusted his neighbour. Vienna, having been ransacked by the Soviet army, was now ruled by the four victorious Allies – the USA, France, the UK and Russia. Out of the sewers came *The Third Man*, Orson Welles, to make a fast buck with watered-down penicillin.

Adolf's Art

Austrian-born Adolf Hitler came to Vienna in 1907, aged 17, to be an artist. The judgement on his work by the Academy of Fine Arts was: 'inadequate'. From then on his book, *Mein Kampf* ('my struggle'), was to be directed against the Jews, Communists, Christians and practically everyone else. The sum of people who eventually died as a result of him was some 25 million. But it was not rejection that motivated him. Neither was he poor. He certainly had sufficient to go to the opera regularly. It's possible that Hitler's fits of rage, blame, depression, wild decisions and violence can be attributed to manic-depression at a time when there was no medication for the disease. Or possibly neurosyphilis, only curable by penicillin and only available in the medical armoury of his Anglo-American enemies.

⭐ See Map D–C1 | ★★

You can still visit several of the places where this film was made and if you are an addict, as many are, then go to **The Third Man Museum** in Pressgasse 25, Margareten's 5th district. Its eight rooms include composer Anton Karas's original zither.

SIGMUND FREUD MUSEUM

At Berggasse 19 you can see the house, now a museum, where Freud lived and the rooms in which he practised what would possibly have been considered, at the time, the 'dark art' of **psychoanalysis**. Between 1900 and 1910 Freud and others may have made Vienna the intellectual centre of the world, but Vienna knew it not. Most of **Freud's possessions**, including his famous couch, he took with him when he fled to London in 1938 to evade the Nazis. But you can see his coat, hat and walking stick, which he left, plus good reproductions of his work and home life. In 1896 Sigmund Freud invented the word 'psychoanalysis' and in 1900 published his *The Interpretation of Dreams*.

Freud died in London a year after escaping the Nazis. He had been ill for many years; now it had become too much for him. His doctor, as agreed between them many years earlier, gave him a lethal dose of morphine.

Third Man Museum
✉ 4 Pressgasse 25
🚇 U4: Kettenbrücken-gasse
☎ (43) 1 586 4872
🖥 www.3mpc.net
🕐 Sat 14:00–18:00 and Tue 18:00–20:00.
💰 Adults: €7.50, children (10–16): €4

Sigmund Freud Museum
✉ Berggasse 19, A–1090 Wien
☎ (43) 1 319 1596
🖥 www.freud-museum.ac.at
✉ office@freud-museum.at
🕐 Open daily 09:00–17:00 (Jun–Sep daily 09:00–18:00). Guided tours by appointment.

Opposite: The Third Man *is a famous British film directed by Carol Reed.*
Below*: The pre-World War II home where Sigmund Freud lived is now a museum on his life.*

SCHÖNBRUNN PALACE

The Grand Tour ticket will take you into the 40 rooms that are open to the public. These include **Maria Theresia's bedroom**, the **Porcelain Room**, **Blue Chinese Salon**, **Napoleon Room** and the **Millions Room**, which got its name because it is said the Kaiserin paid in excess of a million silver florins to have it done up to her liking.

Franz Josef's bedroom is where he died on 21 November 1916. His sombre **study** is next door. The bedroom where Princess Elisabeth, Sisi, supposedly evaded her husband for two nights after their wedding is decorated in blue upholstery.

The 'English' flushing **toilet**, the first of its kind in the palace, is next door.

Empress Maria Theresia apparently held secret meetings with Chancellor Count Wenzel von Kaunitz to discuss strategy and diplomacy during the Seven Years' War with Prussia that ended up involving half of Europe. From his apartments in the Schönbrunn Palace, Kaunitz could apparently reach the **Round Chinese Room** via a secret spiral staircase hidden behind the panelling.

Tickets to Ride

Vienna has an inter-linked transport system. A single daily ticket will get you on and off trams, buses, trains and metro for as long as you like. A weekly ticket, or *Wochenkarte*, costs €12.50. A monthly ticket, or *Monatskarte*, costs €45. You can get on and off and on again, 300 times if you like. Punch your ticket once in the on-board blue box and keep it on you. But everything operates on trust. The Vienna Card costs €18.50 and offers transport plus discounts for visitor attractions, shops and restaurants. Valid for 72 hours. A single-journey ticket costs €1.50. U-Bahn stations have multilingual vending machines, and *Tabak* (tobacconists) also sell tickets.

Opposite: The formal gardens of Schönbrunn belie the fascinating variety of the palace's museums and apartments.
Right: The Great Gallery at Schönbrunn has hosted kings and presidents.

SCHÖNBRUNN GARDENS

In many ways the best way to see and explore Schönbrunn is not to begin with the palace itself but to head for the hilltop **Gloriette**, a high arched folly with a pond at its base. Stark against the horizon, it overlooks the whole sweep of the park and the city beyond. This is where Fischer von Erlach had intended building Austria's Versailles. But money was tight and there were more wars to fight. The stairs up to the central section and observation terrace are lined with delicious monsters, convoluted sculptures whose meaning may have been lost even to their creator. On the same side as the **Tyrolean Garden** and loos, there is a 'Sound of Music' **Lederhosen Café** with great views from the windows.

The surrounding **woods** with their paths, benches and cool dappled sunlight – the walk up to the Gloriette is steep in parts – the woods are a good place to picnic and distance oneself from the madding crowd.

Schönbrunn Palace
✉ Kultur- und
Betriebsges.m.b.H.
Schloss Schönbrunn
A–1130 Wien
☎ (43) 1 81113 239
📠 (43) 1 81113 333
🖥 www.schoenbrunn.at
🕘 Apr–Jun
08:30–17:00,
Jul–Aug 08:30–18:00,
Sep–Oct 08:30–17:00,
Nov–Mar 08:30–16:30.

Schönbrunn Gardens
✉ Herr Wimmer
Schlosspark Schön-
brunn A–1130 Wien
☎ (43) 1 877 5087
📠 (43) 1 877 5067
🖥 www.bundes
gaerten.at
📧 direktion@bgwien.
bmlfuw.at

See Map D–E6 ★★

Above: *Lake and formal gardens lead from the filigreed entrance gates to the Upper Belvedere Palace.*

BELVEDERE

The Upper Belvedere Palace is rather stark and solid, particularly when viewed from the main entrance. It was purpose built for a military man and for the popular masked balls of the time with plenty of open space for fireworks displays. It is much larger than its sister palace down below. In this palace's **Marble Hall**, the Austrian State Treaty of 1955 was signed, granting the country full independence after 10 years of occupation by the World War II Allies. The Hall contains a wonderful collection of Austria's three great Jugendstil modernist painters, Klimt, Schiele and Kokoschka. Here you will see Klimt's most photographed work, the yellow-gold and superbly colourful *The Kiss*, behind glass. It is of himself and his lady, Emilie Flöge.

Near the entrance gates to the Upper Belvedere is the **Alpine Garden**. It was started in 1803, Europe's oldest. It leads into the university's even older **Botanical Garden** flanking the Belvedere.

ZENTRALFRIEDHOF

Not since the ancient Egyptians has anyone done death like the Viennese. Funerals have always been a good opportunity for pomp, circumstance and a beautiful corpse, *eine schöne Leich*. Or, as the **Undertaker's Museum** in Wieden will testify, a 'decent'

Belvedere Palace
⊠ Prinz Eugen Strasse 27
☎ 01 795 57134
🖥 www.belvedere.at
✆ public@belvedere.at

Zentralfriedhof
⊠ Simmeringer Hauptstrasse 230–244
☎ (43) 1 760 41
🖥 www.wien.info
🕘 Nov–Feb 08:00–17:00, Mar, Apr, Sep, Oct 07:00–18:00, May–Aug 07:00–19:00.
🚋 Tram 6, 71: Zentralfriedhof

See Map E–C5 | ★★

burial. The **Central Cemetery** (Zentralfriedhof) in Simmering is huge, Europe's second largest with 3.3 million pampered residents in its tree-lined, red-lanterned graves, memorials and exotic pantheons in an area of 2.5km² (1 sq mile). The cemetery was opened in 1874, replacing the five municipal cemeteries, and ever since has been a place to stroll, tend family graves, pray, water the flowers, chat and picnic.

VIENNA WOODS

The **Wienerwald**, or Vienna Woods, is a 1250km² (482-sq-mile) belt of forest, woodland meadows, hills and streams surrounding Vienna in an arc that stretches from the Kahlenberg hills on the Danube, right round the city's western suburbs to the foothills of Austria's southern Alps. Few cities have a green lung of this magnitude on their suburban doorstep.

This summit of 484m (1537ft) at the northeast edge of the Vienna Woods has a marvellous view over the whole of Vienna, the Danube and as far south as the Schneeberg Alps. **Kahlenberg** is one of two peaks, the other being the slightly lower **Leopoldsberg** (at 425m/1350ft). These two hills changed names in 1693 and, to add to the confusion, Kahlenberg was originally called *Sauberg* because of the plentiful wild boar that are found here.

Below: *A cyclist burning calories near the Vienna Woods.*

See Map B–B3 ★★

Prater Amusement Park

🖥 www.aboutvienna.org/sights/prater.htm
🖥 www.wien.info/prater/index-e.html
🚇 U-Bahn: Praterstern Wien Nord

Wiener Kriminal-museum

✉ Grosse Sperlgasse 24, A–1020.
☎ 214 4678
🖥 www.kriminal museum.at
🚇 U-Bahn: Schwedenplatz

PRATER AMUSEMENT PARK

In Vienna it is the **Riesenrad Giant Ferris Wheel** that defines the city skyline. The Prater amusement park, forests and recreation area in **Leopoldstadt** was opened to the public in 1766 (Prater means a 'plain'). There is jogging, horse-riding, a children's railway, trade fair centre, planetarium, racecourse, tennis clubs and the amusement park with its Ferris wheel made famous in *The Third Man* film.

The **Great Wheel**, designed by British military engineer Walter Basset, initially weighed in at 440 tonnes, with 120 spokes and 30 cars. You get taken 64m (210ft) off the ground, with the wheel revolving in a slight stagger at 75cm (29in) per second, the ride lasting 20 minutes. You can even book a formal evening dinner party in one of the cars.

The long, wide and shady **Hauptallee** (the main avenue) is busy at weekends with hearty fellows and jogger-damsels in designer T-shirts and shades, iPods and ski-sticks. Branch left or right off the Hauptallee and you are immediately into forest, gardens, streams, occasional lakes and loads of wild flowers. Halfway down, near the loos, is a tiny open-bench tearoom, with 1950s music.

See Map D–E1 ★★

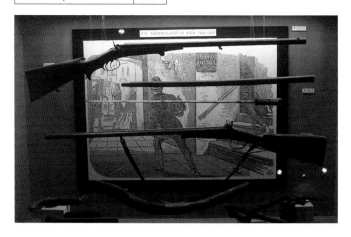

WIENER KRIMINALMUSEUM

The exhibits, often in darkened red silhouette, proceed blood-thirstily from century to century. There are lots of period pictures of knife-wielding felons and public executions, historic police uniforms, 'black' or illegal fishermen, the beginnings of forensic science and a reproduction of 'Instrument F', a sophisticated guillotine introduced to Vienna in 1938 by the Nazis. More than 1000 people were decapitated. There are up-close dagger murders, assassinations, the infamous 'maiden killings' and the graphic lynching of War Minister Latour hanged from a lamp post in the 1848 uprising. Interpol was founded in Vienna in 1923.

There is a **Torture Museum** in Vienna, an **Undertaker's**, or **Death**, **Museum** and a **Criminals Museum**. They are deliciously macabre and perhaps not to everyone's taste. But if you like murder, mayhem and detective fiction, then start with the small house of horrors, Wiener Kriminalmuseum.

Above: *Murder weapons in the Wiener Kriminalmuseum are lit in blood-red.*
Opposite: *The giant Ferris wheel at the Prater Amusement Park has been thrilling visitors for over 100 years.*

Nightline
Midnight strikes in Vienna. The castles of kings and churches of ancients rest in quiet. But still you can get back to your hotel. Between 00:30 and 05:00, every half-hour, buses run on a total of 22 routes. Look out for the small 'N' (the half-asleep night eyes) logo on bus stop timetables.

⭐ *See* Map E   ★

Above: *The hydro-foil, or Schnellboot (fast boat), flashes past en route to Vienna from Budapest.*

CRUISING THE BLUE DANUBE

King **Richard I, the Lionheart** (Coeur de Lion) of England, who reigned 1189–99, was a romantic knight errant in the poetic Camelot days of Sherwood Forest and Robin Hood. Richard took the Cross in 1188 and went on the **Third Crusade**. He could be hot-tempered and made cutting remarks about Leopold of Austria and the Holy Roman Emperor's representative. Shipwrecked on his way home, he was obliged to go overland. He passed through Vienna, was recognized – kings are difficult to disguise – was captured and imprisoned for two years (1192–94) in a hilltop castle overlooking the village of **Dürnstein** on the Danube. This is one of several exceptionally picturesque castles you pass on the **Wachau cruise** from wine-growing **Krems** to **Melk** (*see* page 81), whose Benedictine monastery church is one of the world's most magnificent examples of Baroque art.

The train from Wien Franz Josef's Station takes an hour to get to Krems, passing **Klosterneuburg Monastery** perched on its Vienna Woods mountain. Krems is a wealthy 1000-year-old wine town and port made up of three villages: **Krems**, **Stein** and **Und**. The **Piaristenkirche** tower in Krems used to be the town's lookout post in the days of marauding river brigands.

CRUISING THE BLUE DANUBE

Cruising the Blue Danube
For details on cruising the Danube in Austria, visit the following websites:
🖥 www.travelsignposts.com/Austria/Melk.php and http://eurorivercruises.com/Destinations/danube.htm and www.rivercruising.com

Stein is smaller than Krems and does not have the same traffic. The ruins of the **Minoritenkirche** are 13th century and the **Parish Church**, *Pfarrkirche*, has a traditional Baroque onion dome.

From Krems railway station to the Danube cruise embarkation jetty it is a 20-minute walk via a continuity of riverside paths. In the summer there are usually five daily departures to Melk, starting at 10:00.

Across a wide river plain opposite Krems is the **Göttweig Benedictine Abbey**, founded in 1083 but rebuilt in 1720, with two onion domes. There are some 18 Benedictine monasteries around Vienna that produce a variety of crops, honey, beer, flowers, wine, grapes and fruit. Nearly all of their wonderful gardens can be visited.

The **Danube** is not very wide in the Wachau valley. It flows swiftly through green, steep-rising, sometimes craggy hills of forest and grapevines. It is enormously picturesque, a classic setting for the old medieval *Minnesänger* troubadours who went from castle to castle singing of noble ladies and derring-do in far-off lands.

Left: *Dürnstein castle and village on the Danube.*

Above: *The Ruprechtskirche is considered to be the oldest church in Vienna.*

Places of Worship
Peterskirche

Johann Lukas von Hildebrandt built this Baroque church with its mighty dome in 1703–08. Its twin towers were squeezed by lack of space but the trompe l'oeil interior dripping with gilt and ochre stucco gives the impression that it is much larger than it really is. Check out the fully clothed skeletons of Roman catacomb martyrs in glass coffins. Throughout December the church displays a host of lovely Christmas cribs. Photography is allowed.

✉ *Petersplatz 6*
☎ *01 5336433*
🕐 *07:00–18:00 daily*
🚇 *Stephansplatz*

Ruprechtskirche

The oldest church in Vienna is St Ruprechts, a flight of steps above busy Schwedenplatz and the Danube. Ruprecht was chosen by the Danube boatmen, salt merchants, to be their patron saint. Salt was extremely valuable in medieval times. The small and squat Romanesque ivy-covered church lies on the foundation of an 8th-century church, rebuilt and altered many times. The highly colourful stained glass inside is surprisingly modern and there is an area

34

for exhibitions of art. Photography is allowed. Wheelchair access.

✉ *Ruprechtsplatz*
☎ *01 5356003*
🕐 *09:30–11:30 Mon–Fri, Mass Sat 17:00–18:00, Sun 10:30*
🚊 *Schwedenplatz*

Stadttempel (Synagogue)

Behind St Ruprechts church are little cobbled alleys with small restaurants and elegant high cupolas (an area in the 1980s so packed with bars and lost revellers that it was nicknamed the Bermuda Triangle). It leads to the only Jewish Synagogue to escape the destruction of the 1938 Nazi Kristallnacht. Ironically, throughout World War II the Austrian Resistance (05) had its headquarters in this area at Ruprechtsplatz 5, a stone's throw from the Hotel Metropol's Gestapo torture centre. The Stadttempel's 1820s interior is neoclassical.

To pre-empt any anti-Semitic manifestation, it is patrolled by police.
✉ *Seitenstettengasse 4*
☎ *01 531040*
🕐 *Mon–Thu, by appointment for 11:30 and 14:00 tours (bring passport)*
🚊 *Schwedenplatz*

Augustinerkirche

The last section of the Hofburg is a wing linking the National Library to the Gothic church and monastery of **St Augustin**, with its lovely vaulting. Augustin (AD354–430) was bishop of ancient Hippo (in today's Algeria), one of the fathers of the Christian church. He was apparently something of a gallant in his youth and is credited with saying: '*Lord make me good…. but not yet.*' Augustinerkirche, a Habsburg wedding favourite, has a full orchestra at Sunday high Mass.
✉ *Augustinerstrasse 3*
☎ *01 5337099*
🕐 *08:00–17:00 daily*
🚊 *Stephansplatz*

Votivkirche

You will see the lacy twin spires of the sandstone Votivkirche (Votive church) when you emerge from Schottentor Underground. It was built 130 years ago to launch Kaiser Franz Josef's demolition of the old city walls and the building of a Ringstrasse of grand buildings surrounding his palace. It was also in praise of the Lord for his narrow escape from an assassination attempt by one János Libényi, a Hungarian nationalist and tailor by trade, in the winter of 1853. It is said only a button on his stiff collar saved him from the dagger thrust. Directly opposite the new university, round the corner from Schottentor, is a massive plinth capped by a golden-winged angel. Behind and to the left of this monument, a ramp leads up to part of the old city's medieval star-shaped **Mölker Bastei** ramparts.

Below: *The Karlskirche is situated on the south side of Karlsplatz, Vienna.*

✉ *Rooseveltplatz 8*
☎ *01 4061192*
🕓 *09:00–13:00 and 16:00–18:30 Tue–Sat, 09:00–13:00 Sun.*
🚇 *Schottentor*

Karlskirche

Baroque is a style of decoration and architecture characterized by excessive ornamentation. Any corner, ceiling, wall or altar left bare was, it seemed, an affront to God. The style flourished in Europe from about 1580 to 1720. It certainly hits you between the eyes when you walk into a church like **Karlskirche**. Inside, the magnificent dome's windows bathe the church in light, a glass elevator rising to 47m (154ft) – when restoration is not in progress – enabling one to see the beautiful fresco and artistry of Johann Michael Rottmayer. The whole complex towers over Karlsplatz and looks beautiful from the little garden in front, or washed in pale aquamarine light at night.
✉ *Karlsplatz A–1040*
☎ *7124456*
🕓 *09:00–12:00 and 13:00–17:30 Mon–Sat, 13:00–17:30 Sun.*
🚇 *Karlsplatz*

Servitenkirche

This Baroque church (1651–77), which much influenced the later Peterskirche and Karlskirche, was the only one outside the city walls to survive the onslaught of the Turks in 1683. It is only open, for Mass, early mornings and evenings.
✉ *Servitengasse 9*
☎ *3176195*
🕓 *07:00–09:00 and 18:00–19:00 Mon–Fri, 18:00–20:00 Sat, 07:00–12:00 and 17:00–20:00 Sun.*
🚇 *Rossauer Lände*

Michaelerkirche

There are some fabulous statues of Hercules' labours facing the *platz* that surrounds this 13th-century medieval church. Its façade and interior have been redone in neoclassical and Baroque styles by the doubtful tastes of succeeding generations. The ceiling above the high altar is a sunburst of Rococo alabaster angels and cherubs armed with shields and spears tipped with gold. It has the largest medieval church organ in Vienna, and, a macabre touch, a crypt of skulls, bones and mouldering coffins, some of their inmates still with their boots on.

✉ *Michaelerplatz 1*
☎ *5338000*
🕓 *07:00–18:00 daily*
🚇 *Herrengasse*

Kirche am Steinhof

This colourful Jugendstil church, designed by avant-garde architect Otto Wagner, was completed in 1907 as a chapel for the city's main psychiatric hospital. A little out of town, it has great views. The interior is lit by sparkling mosaic windows.

✉ *Baumgartner Höhe 1*
☎ *910 6011201/4*
🕓 *15:00–16:00 Sat*
🚌 *Tram 48A*

Maria am Gestade

'Am Gestade' means 'by the riverbank' – this 14th-century Gothic church with its prickly filigree tower used to be on a tributary of the Danube, where bargemen offloaded their cargoes. Vienna's patron saint, Klemens Maria Hofbauer, is buried here. In his lifetime he would have marvelled at the Gothic panel paintings of the coronation of the Virgin and the Annunciation angel informing her she was to give birth to the child Jesus.

✉ *Salvatorgasse 12*
☎ *5339594*
🕓 *07:30–18:00 daily, but by appointment*
🚇 *Schwedenplatz*

Museums and Galleries
Jüdisches Museum

This 1989 museum is a state-of-the-art celebration of Vienna's extraordinary and ancient Jewish culture and art, not merely a photographic record of the terrible Shoah, or Holocaust. Holograms, free-standing displays and cleverly woven sound bites follow the enormous – and often unappreciated – contribution the Jews made to Vienna's music, art, literature and every aspect of Viennese life.

✉ *Dorotheergasse 11*
☎ *5350431*
🕓 *10:00–18:00 Sun–Fri, 10:00–20:00 on Thu.*
🚇 *Stephansplatz*

Kunsthistorisches Museum

An opulent Museum of Fine Art and the world's fourth largest collection of priceless paintings. The first floor alone has 15 exhibition rooms. There is even an Egyptian–Oriental selection.

<u>**History of Art**</u>
Rock Art: Southern Africa, Sahara, usually in caves.
Ancient Egypt and Mesopotamia: usually in pyramid tombs.
Ancient Greece: magnificent sculpture, buildings and the body beautiful.
Ancient India: the head of Buddha.
Ancient China: silk scrolls, bamboos.
Islam: intricate detail, Oriental rugs.
Early Middle Ages: Bayeux tapestry.
Renaissance: Jan van Eyck, Botticelli's Venus, Bellini, Dürer, Altdorfer.
Baroque: Caravaggio, Rubens, Van Dyck, Velázquez. Clouds and nymphs.
Revolution: Marat's death by David.
Impressionism: Manet, Monet, Gauguin, Van Gogh.
Modern: Picasso's Spanish Civil War, Guernica.
Postmodern: the bare white canvas with elephant dropping wins top prize.

Opposite: *The Liechtenstein Museum is named after the House of Liechtenstein, one of Europe's oldest noble families.*

The Habsburgs were able to amass these works as their 640-year rule covered half of Europe. *See page 21.*

⌧ *Maria-Therisien Platz*
☎ *525240*
🕐 *10:00–18:00 Tue–Sun, 10:00–21:00 Wed.*
🚇 *Museums Quartier*

Neue Burg Museums

Known as the New Palace because it was only added to the centuries-old complex in 1881–1931, the Neue Burg is home to the Ephesus (Roman antiquities), Musical Instruments, Weapons and Ethnological museums (the latter with a headdress supposedly from Aztec emperor, Moctezuma).

⌧ *Burgring*
☎ *52524484*
🕐 *10:00–18:00 daily, except Tue.*
🚇 *Volkstheater*

Naturhistorisches Museum

Some archaeologists with a sense of fun named the 24,000-year-old Austrian fat lady fertility figure in the museum the Venus of Willendorf. Also on view are Hallstatt Iron Age artefacts, birds of the world, aquarium, meteorites that fell on the Habsburg empire, precious stones and Megarachne, the world's largest fossil spider which, 320 million years ago, was as large as a basketball.

⌧ *Burgring 7*
☎ *52177*
🕐 *09:00–18:00 Mon–Thu, 09:00–21:00 Wed.*
🚇 *Volkstheater*

Wien Museum Karlsplatz

If you want to see works by those colourful turn-of-the-19th-century artists, Carl Moll, Richard Gertsl, Egon Schiele and Gustav Klimt, go to this museum, to the side of Karls-kirche. Klimt's *The Kiss* is probably today the world's most popular poster in the West, replacing Van Gogh's *Sunflowers*.

✉ *Karlsplatz*

☎ *5058747*

🕘 *09:00–18:00, closed on Mondays.*

🚃 *Karlsplatz*

Albertina Museum

The newly refurbished Albertina, southern-most bastion of the Hofburg not far from the opera, forms the final axis of the vast imperial complex. It is a stunning gallery of graphic art and printed works: some 1.5 million, including 65,000 water colours and drawings and 70,000 photographs. There are 145

drawings by Albrecht Dürer (1471–1528), the German master of apocalyptic woodcuts, and 43 by Raphael Santi (1483–1520), the Italian Renaissance painter and architect of today's St Peter's church in Rome.

✉ *Augustinerstrasse 1, Albertinaplatz*

☎ *534830 or 83555*

🕘 *10:00–18:00 daily, open until 21:00 Wed*

🚃 *Karlsplatz or Oper*

Liechtenstein Museum

Fortunately for Vienna the Liechten-stein family have been into art for generations. You can stroll through the picture-lined family

Architecture

New buildings in Vienna have always been hated or loved, but never ignored.
Romanesque: Squat and solid, e.g. St Ruprechts church; 9th–11th centuries.
Gothic: Medieval chur-ches. Pointed arches, ribbed vaulting. Huge spires, e.g. Stephans-dom. Particularly 11th–14th centuries.
Baroque: 17th and 18th centuries, hugely ornate decoration, cupolas, e.g. parts of Hofburg.
Rococo: Over the top Baroque.
Biedermeier: 1815–1848, solid, middle-class. Jewish Stadttempel in the Bermuda Triangle.
Historicism: Architec-ture that copies others, e.g. neo-Baroque, neo-classicism, 19th century.
Jugendstil: stylized and colourful, e.g. Karlsplatz station. Turn of the 19th century.

rooms, admire Friedrich Wilhelm von Schadow's stunning Biedermeier portrait of young Schadow and smile at Peter Fendi's peeping servant girl. You can also buy a package ticket that includes an audio guide, coffee and, quote, 'one piece of cake' in Rubens' Brasserie in the courtyard. The word Biedermeier is a mix of the names of two characters in a popular 19th-century novel.

✉ *Fürstengasse 1*
☎ *31957670*
🕓 *10:00–17:00, except Tue*
🚋 *Friedensbrücke*

Technisches Museum

The energy section in this five-storey museum is fascinating: computer technology, oil drilling (Austria produces oil) and a reconstructed coal mine. There are loads of hands-on activities especially for the children.

Unfortunately there is only one showing a day in the High Voltage Room so book early if you fancy a hair-raising experience. For a double treat day, Vienna's IMAX cinema is next door. The Railway Museum forms part of the Technical Museum.

✉ *Mariahilferstrasse 212*
☎ *899 986000 or 89998*
🕓 *09:00–18:00 Mon–Fri, 10:00–18:00 Sat and Sun.*
🚋 *Zieglergasse*

MAK Museum

The design of this Austrian Museum of Applied Arts is a paean of praise to the country's art and architecture. There is something for everyone, ranging from the first Brentwood rattan chair, the Dubsky Czech porcelain room, the fascinating Wiener Werkstatte Collection – an early 20th-century co-op of artists and

craftspersons – and the quirky Biedermeier Room. The walk-through Historismus Jugendstil is a long screen-changing show. The royal collection of Oriental rugs is barefoot delicious.

✉ *Stubenring 5*
☎ *711360*
🕓 *10:00–00:00 on Tue and 10:00–18:00 Wed–Sun.*
🚋 *Stubentor*

Strassenbahn-museum

The Tramway Museum features 80 of Vienna's venerable red and cream trams, ranging from an 1871 horse-drawn trolley to a still-working steam train. After that came the clanking 'electric' with its controversial overhead wires, the grinding noise of which symbolizes Vienna even today.

✉ *Erdbergstrasse 109*
☎ *7860303*
🕓 *09:00–16:00 Sat–Sun (May–Oct).*
🚋 *Schlachthausgasse*

Left: *The Donner-brunnen fountain (1739) on Neue Markt is regarded as the most important work of the great Baroque sculptor, Georg Raphael Donner.*

ACTIVITIES
Sport and Recreation

There is ice-skating in winter, tobogganing in Vienna's many parks, cross-country skiing along the Prater. In summer there is plenty to jog for: Nordic walking on the Prater Hauptallee or a guided run every Tuesday and Thursday through Vienna's parks, including warm-up and stretching exercises. There are clearly marked routes for mountain biking. One can opt for bungee-jumping, climbing, tennis, inline skating, riding, golf, or, at Schönbrunn Palace, swimming. Choose your sport and contact ⌨ www.wien.info

Soccer

The 2008 UEFA European Football Championship, Euro 2008, took place in Austria and Switzerland. A total of 16 teams participated. Austria and Switzerland automatically qualified as hosts, with Austria making its first appearance in the championships.

Ernst-Happel-Stadium, with its 53,000 seats, is in the huge Prater recreation complex and this is where the final took place. A

The Hills are Alive

The tail end of the Alps is only 90km (60 miles) south from Vienna. There are direct trains to Simmering, whose historic railway was built in 1854. Weaving its way through 31 tunnels and viaducts and beautiful Alpine scenery, it is the first railway to be designated a UNESCO World Heritage Site. The three most popular mountains for both skiing and wandering are Rax, Schneeberg and Simmering. All three have year-round ski lifts. Rax at 2007m (6587ft) has a large 34km (21-mile) plateau, while Schneeberg at 2075m (6810ft) is southern Austria's highest peak. The chalets in the mountains all have stunning views and good restaurants, in particular the 1929 Looshaus in the Mount Rax area. For Information: Tourismusregion Süd-alpin, ☎ (02664) 2539-1, ⌨ www.tiscover.com/noe-sued

Right: *Show off your great aptitude for ice-skating indoors at the Albert Schulz Ice Skating Rink and at the Vienna Civic Centre.*

good many trees around the stadium had to be cut for security reasons. There were other stadiums, expanded and renovated for the event, in Salzburg and Innsbruck. Austria's Hypo-Arena in Carinthia Province was constructed specifically for Euro 2008.

Ice Skating

Come winter, everyone gets out their ice skates and heads for one of the many rinks or even outdoor basketball courts which are conveniently converted to ice-skating rinks when the temperature freezes over. And when it's really cold, the Alte Donau River has mile after mile of perfect ice, all free.

The professional rinks include the **Weiner Eislaufverein**, which at 6000m² (7175 sq yds) is probably the world's largest open-air rink south of the Arctic. Inline skates can be hired at Donauinsel (Copa Kagrana) and the Prater.

Cycling

The long reaches of the Danube, Prater, and the forested hills of the Vienna Woods are the favourites for cycling. Vienna is exceptionally bicycle-friendly with special paths for cyclists in the city, loads of bicycle-hire depots (bring your credit card) and a public transport system that caters for cyclists. Get a copy of *Stadtplan Wien für Radfahrer Innen* with its detailed maps of cycle paths and cycle tours in Vienna.

Dancing

The summer dance festival, July–August, offers among other delights rock'n'roll lessons while the winter equivalent (February–March) includes jazz dance at the University Sports Centre, Schmelz. The grand Vienna Opera Ball (men in tails, women in white dresses) is held on the last Thursday before Ash Wednesday (Easter), Vienna's Carnival week (*Weiner Festwochen*) of music. It is preceded by the Opera House ballet performance of *Die Fledermaus* shown on a huge screen in Stephansplatz. There are balls or fancy dress dances at the Rathaus, Musikverein and the Hofburg. No invitations – just buy a ticket as you do on New Year's Eve at the Neue Burg. Check with the special calendar printed by the Vienna Tourist Office, ☎ 24555 or 211140.

Golf

There are at least a dozen clubs in Vienna including the 18-hole Golf Club Wein (oldest one in Austria) in the forested Prater.

Climbing

A particularly unusual climbing wall can be found at the *Kletteranlage Flaktürme*, the old World War II Nazi anti-aircraft tower, a huge concrete monstrosity in Esterházypark. Organized by the Austrian Alpen-

---

Skiing Slopes
Most skiing is in the Austrian Alps. But if that is too far, try:
Skianlage Hohe Wand
⊠ 14, Mauerbachstrasse 172–174, in the Vienna Woods, when snow has fallen to bond with daily manmade spraying.
☎ 9791057
🕘 Dec–Mar
09:00–21:30 daily
🚌 Bus No. 249, 250
💰 €14

Skianlage Dollweise
⊠ 13, Ghelengasse 44, Lainzer Tiergarten (400m/435yd slope)
🕘 10:00–dusk daily
🚌 Bus No. 54B, 55B

Beaches
There are many small beaches on both the Vienna Danube Island and Lobau shore.
Krapfenwaldbad,
✉ 19 Krapfenwald-gasse 65–73
☎ 3201501
🕐 May–Sep 09:00–20:00 daily
🚌 Bus 38A
🛥 Donauinsel
Schaftberg,
✉ Josef-Redi-Gasse 2
☎ 4791593
Strandbad Alte Donau, ✉ 22 Arbeiter-strandbadstrasse, 91
☎ 2636538
🛥 Alte Donau
✉ **Thermbad Oberlaa**, Kudbad-strasse 14
☎ 680099600
🕐 09:00–22:00
🚌 67

verrein, there are 20 routes, with gradients of 4–8 and rising to a maximum height of 34m (113ft). ☎ 5854748.

Keeping Fit
There are no fewer than nine *Club Danube* gyms in Vienna. ☎ 7988400.

Sport of Kings
Vienna's top horse-racing track is at the southernmost point of the Prater, Fradenau. ☎ 7289531 for fixtures and track events.

Alternative Vienna
The Undertaker's Museum has a cord and bell device that could be rung from inside your grave if you felt you were not quite dead. But there was no such luck for those buried in the Nameless Ones Cemetery, **Friedhof der Namenlosen**, near the waters of the Alberner Harbour, on the southern outskirts of the city. One hundred years ago, the swirling waters of the river curved

Below: *The Nameless Ones Cemetery.*

and twisted here, throwing up a grizzly harvest of bodies: men, women and children who had committed suicide, were perhaps murdered or drowned – the lost nameless ones of the Danube. This is their last little graveyard. It is a poignant and lonely spot with a Dickensian feel to it. There are a total of 104 graves marked by iron crosses. A few of the graves have names but there are many that are marked *Namenlos,* or Nameless. The graves are well looked-after. There's a pillbox **chapel**, a lovely poem etched on a plaque at the entrance, and a slot in which to drop a coin or two for flowers.

Above: *The Pestsäule is located on Graben, a street in the inner city of Vienna.*

Walking Tours

Walking is by far the best way to experience Vienna. There seems to be a surprise around every corner in this compact little city. Keep an eye over your left shoulder when you're crossing the roads. Do not jaywalk. Cars will normally give way to you at a zebra crossing even when there are no lights. Politeness is a Viennese thing.

Conducted by knowledgeable and professional Austrian guides, these tours can include the **1683 Turkish Siege**, the **Old City**, or the **Homes of Mozart, Beethoven and Schubert**. One of the most fascinating is the '**1000 Years of Jewish Tradition**'. Then there is *fin-de-siècle* **Vienna** and **Sigmund Freud**, or **Unknown Underground Vienna**, or **Vienna, Capital of Music**.

One alternative is to start at the Staatsoper, heading north along Kärntner Strasse which becomes a pedestrian mall lined with luxurious shops and cafés. Then go down Marco-d'Aviano-Gasse towards Neue Markt and the Kaisergruft Crypt in the

Pilgrims' Progress
When April arrives it is time for Christian women and men to go on pilgrimage. The 14th-century English poet Geoffrey Chaucer would probably not have recognized today's Danube pilgrims. But the practice is no different: walking, praying, staying overnight at an inn. The Jacobsweg route along the Danube northwest of Vienna, through forest and hills and clearly signposted, covers a distance of 800km (497 miles). Some walk alone, some go by bicycle. Some even hitch a ride in a Danube leisure boat. There's a book mapping the route: *Auf dem Jacobsweg durch Österreich* by Peter Lindenthal.

Right: *The Danube cycle track opened in the 1980s. It is excellent for families with children, and does in fact attract many families.*

Opposite: *If you prefer a more leisurely way of getting around Vienna, the best way would be in a horse-drawn cab known as a* fiaker.

Capuchin church. Heading back to Kärntner Strasse, you will come to Stephansplatz and Gothic cathedral. Pause to enjoy the statue actors and musicians before strolling down the Graben past the twirly golden Plague Column, or Pestsäule, then turn left into Kohlmarkt to magnificent Michaelerplatz, entrance to the Hofburg Palace and its many historic delights. The Neue Burg Palace looks over the equestrian statues and the Volksgarten. If you are not too exhausted, take a ride around the palace, past the Royal Burggarten to the Victorian Palm House and then Albertina Museum. You could lunch at Café Mozart or Sacher's before proceeding back to Oper.

Organized Tours

Nostalgic Tram

Every Saturday, ☺ 11:30 and 13:30, May to early October, you can take a ride around many of Vienna's historic sites on an old-time tram tour. It also operates on Sundays with extra departures at ☺ 09:30. You leave from the Karlsplatz/Otto Wagner Pavilions and the tour takes an hour.

Ride on the Wild Side
Bike routes are clearly marked in green Donau-Radwanderweg signs – if you fancy cycling the three hours from Krems to Melk – the best way to see local folk, their villages and sample their wines. For more detailed information, get hold of Rick Steves' annual *Germany, Austria and Switzerland.*

Bicycle Hire

There are 500km (311 miles) of cycle paths in Vienna and 50 city bike stations. Rent them using your credit card whenever you see the sign of the red and yellow cyclist, and at the main railway stations. You can take your bike on the S-Bahn and U-Bahn, but not at rush hour. The fare for the bike is 50% of your normal fare.

Fiaker Hackney Cab

You'll see these lovely horse-drawn cabs at Albertina Platz (museum near Mozart Café), Michaelerplatz (Hofburg entrance), Heldenplatz (Hitler's favourite balcony) and Stephansplatz (cathedral). The cabbies will take you for a ride for a mere €60 for 40 minutes, hopefully with English dialogue.

Boating

DDSG is shorthand for one of those gorgeous German names: *Donaudampfschifffahrtsgesellschaft*. These cruise boats on the Danube Canal, one of four arms of the Danube and the one nearest the old city,

Tours

City Bus Tours: try Vienna sightseeing tours, ☎ (01) 7124 6830, 🖳 www.vienna sightseeingtours.com You can combine these tours with Vienna Boys' Choir and Spanish Riding School. Another option is the 'Red Vienna' (1920–30) tour to buildings such as Karl Marx Hof.

Danube Boat Trips: DDSG at Schwedenplatz. 🖳 www.ddsg-blue-danube.at Short upriver trips or go to Bratislava and Budapest.

Music Mile Vienna: for Western classical music fans, ☎ (01) 58830-0. 🖳 www.musikmeile.at

Architecture Old & New for building buffs: 🖳 www.azw.at (Architekturzentrum Wien).

Third Man Tour: possibly the best of all. Go by metro (U-Bahn) to the many locations of post WWII Vienna where the iconic 1949 film *Der Dritte Mann* was filmed. And with luck, take a peep into the old sewers where the final chase took place. Wien-Tourismus, ☎ (01) 774 8901, 🖰 info@vienna walks.com Tours approximately every four days.

Walking Tours: Vienna Walks & Talks, ☎ (01) 774 8901, 🖳 www.viennawalks.tix.at

leave from hectic Schwedenplatz for short trips upriver. You can also do an evening Johann Strauss cruise or, if you're Australian, the Spare Ribs Fahrt. There are cruises on the picturesque Wachau section of the Danube to Melk and others to Bratislava. There is also a hydrofoil to Budapest and a 12-day cruise from Amsterdam to Vienna in the summer.

Fun for Children

Vienna is very child-friendly and there are attractions specifically for children, including the **Puppet Theatre** in Schönbrunn, the **Technical Museum's** adventure area, the funfair and giant Ferris wheel at **Prater**, the **Schönbrunn zoo** (and maze), **ZOOM Children's Museum** and **Haus des Meeres** (sharks, snakes and piranhas in an aquarium built inside a former World War II Nazi flak tower). **Schönbrunn Palace** has special tours for children (cakes being made for the royal children), the **Butterfly House** (Schmetterlinghaus) in the Burggarten's Greenhouse, and finally there is an **Adventure Swimming Pool** (Dianabad Tropicana) with Pirates of the Caribbean and a waterslide.

Donau Park

The **Donau Park** occupies most of the middle section of the island between the **New Danube** and the **Old Danube**. Orientate yourself by walking from the Alte Donau (U1) towards the 252m (828ft) **Danube Radio Tower** with its two revolving restaurants and viewing terrace reached by express lift. There are children's playgrounds and pony rides, peaceful lily-lakes, apocalyptic sculptures by Karl Wolf and banks of patterned flowers.

Danube Tower
The Donauturm in the Danube Park was built in 1964. Weighing in at 17,600 tons, it stands 252m (830ft) high, and has two revolving restaurants reached by a lift which takes 35 seconds to get there. The Lookout Terrace is a mere 150m (490ft) high. The huge red wave on the top is the Austria Bank logo. The tower and park face the Old Danube, or in the publicity brochures, 'die schöne Alte Donau'. Here, there are 8km (5 miles) of sailing schools, rowboats to hire, pedal boats, restaurants, special music and firework events, and all sorts of children's activities.

Left: *The Prater amusement park is in the second district of Vienna, Leopoldstadt. The best-known attraction is the Riesenrad Ferris wheel. The park also features rides, bumper cars, carousels and more.*

The Isola Beer Garden sits at the foot of the huge tower.

The Prater Amusement Park
In Vienna it is the **Riesenrad Giant Ferris Wheel** that defines the city skyline. Children love the Prater amusement park with it's many activities. For more details, *see* Highlights, page 30.

Museums
Thirty-four of Vienna's plethora of museums have programmes especially for children. They include the Museum Detective at the Museum of Fine Arts, Hoher Markt's Roman Ruins, Overnight Camp-in at the Technical Museum, Ocean Fantasy in ZOOM's underwater world, Austria's navy tour in the Military Museum, afternoon games at the Upper Belvedere Palace, the history of eating, drinking and sleeping at the MAK, and at Vienna's colourful museum, Kunsthaus Wien, youngsters get a 'kiddie bag' to design their own Hundertwasser House.

Above: *The Mariahilferstrasse.*
Opposite: *A shopping area in Graben.*

Food for the Volk

In medieval times, on market day, a flag would be raised. Until noon the only people allowed to purchase from the various markets were courtiers, clergy and citizens. Everyone else had to wait. The streets around Stephansdom reflect the food-oriented priorities of the populace at a time when famine was not uncommon. There is the *Fleischmarkt* (Meat Market), *Kohlmarkt* (Cabbage Market) where today designer brands are sold, *Bauermarkt* (Farmers' Market) and *Getreidemarkt* (Grain Market).

Shopping

Vienna is one of the oldest cities in Europe, and until 100 years ago it had been the power centre of the Habsburg empire that ruled that continent for 640 years. Art, music, architecture and commerce flourished, while from all over the empire came the products of industry, creativity and the skills of the best craftspersons. Consequently Vienna is a wealthy city. Anything found in London, Dubai, Shanghai or New York can be sourced in Vienna's stores. The difference is that in Vienna, visitors can shop in a setting of unsurpassed historical elegance: old-world cafés, Gothic cathedrals, hackney cabs and cobbled streets.

Shops

Antiques

Das Kunstwerk

Art Deco, Jugendstil by Austrian designers Otto Wagner, Adolf Loos, Thonet and Kohn.

✉ *Operngasse 20*
🕐 *11:00–18:00*
🚇 *U-Bahn 2, Karlsplatz*

Dorotheum

Altwaren Auctions (Old Wares Auctions). There are gems to be found among the plethora of up-market must-haves in this, one of Europe's largest auction houses. The Verkauf section is a vast antiques gallery. You can get an agent to bid for you if you like.
✉ *Dorotheergasse 17*
☎ *51560*
🕐 *10:00–18:00 and 17:00 Sat*

Books

Shakespeare & Co
✉ *Starngasse 2*
☎ *5355053*
🕐 *09:00–21:00 Mon–Fri and 19:00 on Sat*
🚋 *Tram 1 or 2*

British Bookshop
Largest selection of English books in Vienna. Many shops stock English books.
✉ *Weiburggasse 24*
☎ *512 19 45*
🕐 *09:30–18:30 Mon–Fri and 18:00 Sat*
🚋 *Tram 1 or 2*

Cameras and Film

Any of many branches of **Niedermyer** (e.g. U2 Schottentor). Good second-hand stock.

Orator
✉ *Westbahnstrasse 23*
☎ *5261010*
🕐 *09:00–18:30 Mon–Fri and 10:00–13:00 Sat*

Confectionery

Lollipop
✉ *Burggasse 57*
Oberlaa
✉ *Neue Markt 16*
Opern Confiserie
✉ *Kärntnerstrasse 47*
Altmann & Kühne
✉ *Graben 30*

Computers (fixing)

Der Computer Doctor
✉ *Gentzgasse 9*
🚇 *Volksoper U6*

Cosmetics

Douglas
There are branches throughout the city (e.g. Graben 29).
Bipa
Visit any Bipa outlet for health and beauty products.

Fashion and Accessories

Vienna Bag
✉ *Bäckerstrasse 7*
☎ *5131184*
Mühlbauer Hats
✉ *Seilergasse 10*
☎ *5122241*
Palmers (men's and women's underwear)
✉ *Kärntnerstrasse 4*
☎ *5129341*

Opposite: Starting mid-November, the Advent season descends upon Vienna. The aromas of candied fruits, cotton candy and other delicacies like Christmas punch and roasted chestnuts wafting around the small wooden market stalls still retain their magical power.

Below*: Mostly Mozart is an extraordinary store located in downtown Vienna where you can find gifts and souvenirs all relating to Mozart and his incredible life.*

Wolford (hosiery and swimsuits)
✉ *Kärntnerstrasse 29*
☎ *5128731*
Art Up (contemporary and Jugendstil)
✉ *Bauernmarkt 8*
☎ *5355097*
Song (cutting-edge gear)
✉ *Landskrongasse 2*
☎ *5322858*
Polyklamott (good second-hand clothes)
✉ *Hofmühlgasse 6*
☎ *9690337*
There are specialist glove, shoe, lederhosen shops and many others.

Good Value (Department Stores)
Steffl
✉ *Kärntnerstrasse 19*

Billa chain
Woolworth
Schlosshoferstrasse
✉ *3 5 Floritsdorf*
🚈 *near Floritsdorf U-Bahn station*

Food
Babettes (food, cookbooks and spices)
✉ *Schleifmühlgasse 17, Wieden*
☎ *5855165*
🚌 *59A*
Manner (wafers and cream delights)
✉ *Stephansplatz 7*
🕐 *10:00–21:00 Mon–Sat.*
And next door:
Bobby's Food Store (imported UK and USA favourites – Marmite and Hersheys)
Meinl am Graben (Vienna's Fortnum and Mason; exotic nibbles and veggies from everywhere – buy organic and feel good)
✉ *Am Graben 19*
Anker (bakery chain with hundreds of branches; get a cup of coffee at most outlets).
Schönbichler (for 101 types of tea and malt whiskies)
✉ *Wollzeile 4*

Cullinarium Österreich
✉ Neue Markt 10–11
☎ 513 82 81

Spar Gourmet
(food chain store)

Jewellery
Köchert
Former jewellers to the Imperial Court. A price distinction proudly remembered when you purchase emeralds for your beloved.

Bernsteinzimmer
Bernstein means 'amber', usually from Poland, something the Romans lusted after 2000 years ago when they invaded Austria.
✉ Seilergasse 19

Chocolates
Truffles at Café Central's **Chocshop** around the corner from the café.

Xocolat
✉ Freyung arcade

Wine
Wein & Co. (chain)
There's a store and deli near the Naschmarkt; another at:
✉ Jasomirgottstrasse 3–5
🕐 10:00–00:00 daily

Böhle (plus deli)
✉ Wollzeile 30
🚇 U-Bahn Stubentor

Music
Black Market
✉ Gonzagasse 9
🕐 at midday

Virgin Megastore
(Austria's largest music store)
✉ Mariahilferstrasse 37

Rave Up
✉ Hofmühlgasse 1

Tenchfler
✉ Windmühlgasse 10

Toys
Spielzeugschachtel
✉ Rauhensteingasse 5

Spielzung
(fascinating range of dollhouse accessories)
✉ Ringstrasse Galerien, Kärntnerring 5–13

Markets

Naschmarkt: half a mile of fruit, cheeses, wines, spices, olives, kebabs, fish restaurants, falafels, sauerkraut, and 24 varieties of vinegar at one kiosk.

Freyung: all organic produce. Executions were held here in medieval times.

Flohmarkt: (Kettenbrückengasse) junk, antiques, 'Roman' coins, clothes, records.

Brunnenmarkt: huge street market, stall holders are mainly Turkish or Balkan.

Karmetifermarkt: loads of kosher food.

Christmas markets (Christkindlmärkte): Rathausplatz (bit kitsch but great for kids), Spittelberg (quality crafts, great atmosphere), Alte Akh (students).

Horse-drawn sleighs, concerts, lots of tat and crowded glühwein (hot, spicy après-ski wine) stalls where everybody is a long-lost friend.

Right: *The Sacher, as the Viennese call it, is a five-star Vienna hotel. It was founded by Eduard Sacher in 1876.*

Imperial Hotel

Doffing his top hat, the green-and-black jacketed concierge ushers you in. The foyer is dazzling in its fretted wood, marble, chandeliers, gilt and hint of cigar smoke. Built in 1863 as a city residence, or *palais*, for the Duke of Württenberg, it was sold, converted into a luxury hotel and opened by the Emperor Franz Josef in 1873. Its guest list of kings and presidents and film stars is unequalled. Hitler stayed here in 1938, as did Mussolini in 1943, hussled in through the back door, having been rescued from Italian partisans. Outside, it faces a huge avenue of Elysian Field lime trees along the Ringstrasse. The Baroque *Fürsten* suite is all blue and gold, with palms, chaise longues, period furniture, chandeliers, massive drapes, Persian rugs and mirrors. If you need to ask the price, you can't afford it (actually, it costs €4500 a night).

WHERE TO STAY

The most expensive and old elegant five-star hotels such as the Bristol, Palais Coburg, Imperial or Sacher do not come cheap. However, they are exquisitely turned out with all the decor trimmings of elegance, taste and opulence. The numerous pensions, on the other hand, are far cheaper and sometimes superior to hotels. There are lots of camping options in the summer, young people's hostels, and rooms in private houses. If you are prepared to go a little out of town, into the suburbs, you will find some gorgeous gems such as the Garten Hotel in Glanzing. Prices depend on the season, high being April–October and the two weeks over Christmas and New Year. The week up to Lent tends to be booked up, but July–August can see lower prices as the theatres and opera close for the holidays. You can always ask for a discount, even if this is received with amusement in high season. For more information and to book online, go to www.vienna.info or www.tiscover.com

Old City (Innere Stadt)

• *LUXURY*

Ambassador

(*see* Map D–D3)
The Opera, Musikverein and Hofburg are only minutes away. Kärtner Strasse is one of Vienna's most prestigious shopping streets.
⊠ 1010 Wien
Kärntnerstrasse 22
☎ (01) 961610
💻 www.ambassador.at

Hotel Bristol

(*see* Map D–D4)
Built in 1892. Lots of original furnishings. Excellent symbiosis of antique elegance and modern hotel technology.
⊠ 1015 Wien,
Kärntnerring 1
☎ (01) 515160
💻 www.luxury
collection.com/bristol

Hotel Imperial

(*see* Map D–E4)
A historical palace since 1863. Original furnishings. Butler service for suite guests. Impressive list of famous guests, including heads of state. Probably most

expensive hotel in Vienna.
⊠ 1015 Wien,
Kärntnerring 16
☎ (01) 501100
💻 www.luxury
collection.com/imperial

Palais Coburg

(*see* Map D–E3)
Luxury all-suite hotel in an antique city palace with a modern luxury touch. There are 35 individually designed suites. Exquisite restaurant with an outstanding selection of wine.
⊠ 1010 Wien,
Coburgbastei 4
☎ (01) 518180
💻 www.palais-
coburg.com

Hotel Sacher

(*see* Map D–D3)
Founded as a hotel in 1876, privately managed since then. One of the most prestigious hotels of Vienna. Relaxing spa refuge. Home of the famous jam-filled, dark chocolate Sachertorte.
⊠ 1010 Wien,
Philarmonikerstrasse 4
☎ (01) 514560
💻 www.sacher.com

Vienna Marriott Hotel

(*see* Map D–E3)
Marriott service combined with Viennese hospitality. The full range of facilities can be found at this business hotel.
⊠ 1010 Wien,
Parkring 12a
☎ (01) 515180
💻 www.vienna
marriott.com

• *MID-RANGE*

Austria Trend Hotel Rathaus Park

(*see* Map D–C1)
A beautiful *palais* near the new city hall and Burg Theatre. The hotel is the former residence of Austrian *fin-de-siècle* writer Stefan Zweig (*Letter from an Unknown Woman*).
⊠ 1010 Wien,
Rathausstrasse 17
☎ (01) 404120
💻 www.austria-
trend.at/rhw

Mailberger Hof

(*see* Map D–D3)
Small family-run hotel in the city centre. Double rooms from

€90 per person.
✉ 1010 Wien,
Annagasse 7
☎ (01) 5120641
▭ www.mailberger
hof.at

Museums Quartier Area

• **MID-RANGE**

Falkensteiner Hotel Am Schottenfeld

(*see* Map D–A3)
A young and innovatively designed hotel. Not too far from the Volkstheater.
✉ 1070 Wien,
Schottenfeldgasse 74
▭ www.falken
steiner.com

Arcotel Wimberger

(*see* Map D–A4)
Great diversity of people, artists, globetrotters, business guests. Close to Mariahilferstrasse, Museums Quartier and Spittelberg. Popular for conventions.
✉ 1070 Wien,
Neubaugürtel 34–36
☎ (01) 521650
▭ www.arcotel.at

• **BUDGET**

Believe It Or Not Hostel

(*see* Map D–A3)
Tiny friendly hostel set in a large private apartment. No groups. Fully equipped kitchen, free internet access, no curfew, cheap beds. Age limit is 17–30 years.
✉ 1070 Wien,
Myrthengasse 10/
apt. 14
☎ (01) 5264658
▭ www.believe-it-or-
not-vienna.at

Schönbrunn Palace Area

• **LUXURY**

Courtyard by Marriott Wien Schönbrunn

(*see* Map D–A6)
Modern hotel next to Schönbrunn Palace. Comfortable rooms, mini-gym.
✉ 1120 Wien,
Schönbrunner
Schlosstrasse 38–40
☎ (01) 8101717

• **MID-RANGE**

Renaissance Wien Hotel

(*see* Map D–A6)
Elegant ambience.

Panorama pool and fitness centre.
✉ 1150 Wien, Linke
Wienzeile/
Ullmannstrasse 71
☎ (01) 891020

Altwienerhof

(*see* Map D–A6)
Not far from Westbahnhof station.
✉ 1150 Wien,
Herklotzgasse 6
☎ (01) 8926000
▭ www.altwiener
hof.at

Wooded & Green Areas

• **MID-RANGE**

Austria Trend Hotel Schloss Wilhelminenberg

(*see* Map E–F2)
Castle hotel on the western edge of the city. Wonderful view over the city. Lovely green location. Part of large chain.
✉ 1160 Wien,
Savoyenstrasse 2
☎ (01) 4858503
▭ www.austria-
trend.at/wiw

Landhaus Fuhrgassl Huber

(*see* Map D–C1)

Traditional Heuriger or Viennese wine tavern, located in the vineyards around Neustift am Walde. Quiet, comfortable rooms with stylish ambience.
⊠ *1190 Wien, Rathstrasse 24*
☎ *(01) 4402714*
🖥 *www.fuhrgassl-huber.at*

Gartenhotel Glanzing

(see Map D–C1)
Charming, four generations family-run hotel in a quiet, exclusive, neighbourhood. Spring to autumn the house is overgrown with wild grapevines. Easy public transport access to the city centre. Recommended.
⊠ *1190 Wien, Glanzinggasse 23*
☎ *tel: (01) 4704272*
🖥 *www.gartenhotel-glanzing.at*

• *BUDGET*
Hostel Hütteldorf

(see Map D–A6)
Quiet location en route to Vienna Woods. Free lockers. Table tennis, billiards.

⊠ *1130 Wien, Schlossberggasse 8*
☎ *(01) 8771501*

Naschmarkt Area
• *MID-RANGE*
Austria Trend Hotel Ananas

(see Map D–B6)
Right next to Naschmarkt and Secession. Good facilities for groups.
⊠ *1050 Wien, Rechte Wienzeile 93–95*
☎ *(01) 546200*

Small Luxury Hotel Das Tyrol

(see Map D–C4)
Boutique hotel on Mariahilferstrasse, Vienna's longest shopping street.
⊠ *1060 Wien, Mariahilferstrasse 15*
☎ *(01) 5875415*
🖥 *www.das-tyrol.at*

Hotel Carlton Opera

(see Map D–C5)
Art Nouveau hotel in a central location.
⊠ *1040 Wien, Schikanedergasse 4*
☎ *(01) 5875302*
🖥 *www.carlton.at*

Schlössel and Garden
There are not many small hotels that have a Bösendorfer grand piano in the lounge, gazed upon by a life-size *Jugendstil* Cleopatra and potted palms. The Gartenhotel in Pötzleinsdorf is one such hotel. It has been run by the same family for four generations. Viennese-born British philosopher Sir Karl Popper was once a guest. Pötzleinsdorf overlooks slopes of vines and, further, the Vienna Woods. Geymüllerschlössel private residence museum, with its collection of 160 antique Viennese clocks, is just up the hill, opposite the tiny and beautifully kept village church.

Divine Laughter

Mozart lived at 20 different addresses in Vienna but the only one to survive is at Domgasse 5, not far from Stephansdom. It is now a museum called, naturally, Mozarthaus. His apartment consisted of four large rooms, two small ones and a kitchen. The four-storey museum features a '*Figaro*' Room, a '*Don Giovanni*' Room, an exhibition floor called '*Vienna in the era of Mozart*' and, on the first floor, *Mozart's apartment* itself. There are three multimedia programmes: '*Mozart's arrival in Vienna*', '*Mozart's residences in Vienna*', and '*The Magic Flute – the Divine Laughter*'.

Liechtenstein Museum Area

• *MID-RANGE*

Arcotel Boltzmann

(*see* Map D–C1)

Popular neighbourhood close to the American embassy.

⊠ *1090 Wien, Boltzmanngasse 8*

☎ *(01) 316120*

🖳 *www.arcotel.at/ boltzmann*

Hotel Mozart

(*see* Map D–B1)

Not far from the Danube Canal. Double rooms from €44 per person.

⊠ *1090 Wien, Julius-Tandler-Platz 4*

☎ *(01) 3172477*

🖳 *www.hotelmozart-vienna.at*

Belvedere Palace Area

• *MID-RANGE*

Hotel Artis Wien

(*see* Map D–F5)

Comfortable city hotel. A modern palace including some rooms with water beds.

⊠ *1030 Wien, Rennweg 51*

☎ *(01) 71325210*

🖳 *www.artis.at*

NH Belvedere

(*see* Map D–F5)

Renovated Art Nouveau building in a quiet area surrounded by embassies. View of the Belvedere Palace and Botanical Garden.

⊠ *1030 Wien, Rennweg 12a*

☎ *(01) 20611*

🖳 *www.nh-hotels.com*

Mariahilfer Shops Area

• *BUDGET*

Wombat's City Hostel Vienna

(*see* Map D–A5)

Very clean, free lockers, free use of the guest kitchen. No age limit, no curfew.

⊠ *1060 Wien, Mariahilferstrasse 137*

☎ *(01) 8972336*

Hostel Ruthensteiner

(*see* Map D–A5)

Non-smoking hostel close to Westbahnhof. Free use of kitchen and BBQ-area. Beautiful garden.

⊠ *1150 Wien, Robert Hamerlinggasse 24*

☎ *(01) 8934202*

Here and There

• MID-RANGE

Renaissance Penta Vienna Hotel

(see Map D–F5)
Hotel from the times of the monarchy in a former military riding school. Near Stadtpark.
✉ 1030 Wien, Ungargasse 60
☎ (01) 711750
💻 www.renaissance hotels.com/VIESE

Hotel Stefanie

(see Map D–E1)
A traditional hotel quite near the Augarten where the Vienna Boys' Choir go to school. It is known for its many years of personal atmosphere and service.
✉ 1020 Wien, Taborstrasse 12
☎ (01) 211500
💻 www.schick-hotels.com

• BUDGET

Hotel Cyrus

(see Map D–E6)
Close to the metro, 10 minutes to the city centre. Free internet access.

✉ 1100 Wien, Laxenburgerstrasse 14
☎ (01) 6022578

Blue Corridor Hostel

(see Map D–B4)
Great location in the hippie Biedermeier neighbourhood of Spittelberg. Surrounded by restaurants and bars. Age limit of 45 years. Above that, presumably, one is on the shelf.
✉ 1070 Wien, Siebensterngasse 15
☎ (0676) 4919231

Hotel Geblergasse

(see Map D–A1)
Close to public transport. Web access in the rooms as well as 24-hour check-in.
✉ 1170 Wien, Geblergasse 21
☎ (01) 4063366

Westend City Hostel

(see Map D–A5)
Rooms with bunk beds, lockers, showers and a 24-hour reception with international crew.
✉ 1060 Wien, Fügergasse 3
☎ (01) 5976729

• APARTMENTS

Mondial Appartement Hotel

(see Map D–B1)
There are 16 apartments partly furnished with antiques.
✉ 1090 Wien, Alserbachstrasse/ Pfluggasse 1
☎ (01) 3107180
💻 www.mondial.at

Appartement Pension 700m zum Ring

(see Map D–C1)
Central location not far from Schottentor station. Great for families.
✉ 1090 Wien, Van-Swieten-Gasse 8
☎ (01) 409 36 80
💻 www.mrhotels.at

Belvedere Apartments

(see Map D–F6)
Serviced apartments for 1–6 persons next to Belvedere Palace.
✉ 1030 Wien, Fasangasse 18
☎ (01) 7984499
💻 www.belv.at
💰 Price range: €18–25 and above; €12–18; €12 and below.
US$1 = €0.74 (2007)

Above: *Vienna is world famous for its coffee and cafés.*

Qahwah For Two
Qahwah is the Arabic word for coffee, of which there are 100 different types. It may actually have originated in Ethiopia. Coffee from Mocha, the seaport in Yemen, is the most prized. When the Turks invaded Vienna 400 years ago, the gift they left was coffee. Try one of these:

Brauner: large or small, black coffee with just a touch of milk.
Biedermeier: Grosse Brauner with a shot of Biedermeier (eggnog with apricot flavour).
Einspänner: small black coffee in a long glass with whipped cream.
Mélange: equal measures of coffee and frothed milk, like an Italian cappuccino.
Schwarzer: small black coffee.
Mazagran: iced coffee and rum. Swallow in one go.

EATING OUT

There are midweek and Saturday food markets all around Vienna's suburbs but the biggest and the busiest is the Nasch-markt located off Karlsplatz. Its long avenues of stalls and eateries are packed with folk hunting fruit, spices, fish, cheese and deli offerings. One breezy stall holder – 'Fast and Furious' on his T-shirt – shouts 'It's free!' Before you can blink, he starts filling up a little container with olives and cheesy snacks. Of course, only your last morsel is actually free.

Coffee to Go, Coffee to Stay

For many, café culture is the most delightful aspect of the Viennese laid-back lifestyle.

The word coffee comes to us via Italian, Turkish, and ultimately the Arabic word *qahwah* (*see* panel), which strangely also means 'wine'.

In Vienna there is a saying that guests at cafés are emigrants, exiles escaping from everyday life in the cosy atmosphere where writers, musicians and artists argue politics, religion and philosophy. You don't have to be literary. Just sit, keep drinking and read the many multi-language newspapers for free.

In the grand old cafés, you can order coffee prepared in some 20 different ways. Coffee upside-down, or *Kaffee Verkehrt*, is hot foamed milk with espresso served in a glass, the *Verlängerter* is a stretched espresso with cream and Cointreau. Then we get into the cakes and meal menus, and lengthy lists of steady-your-nerves-before-commuting-home wines, beers and spirits. Go into **Café Central** in the inner city, wait until you are allocated a table (smoking or non), hand your coat over for hanging up, select a paper, order your favourite, and people-watch for an hour or two while the pianist or violinist plays a little Schubert. True Viennese style.

The best grand cafés include **Sperl** (the 19th-century décor remains unchanged), **Landtmann**, **Hawelka** and **Weimar**. If needs must, you can also buy an inexpensive coffee-to-go at underground stations.

What to Eat

Wiener Schnitzel when it comes in very thin *schnitzel*, or slices, of veal is scrumptious, a bit filling otherwise. The **strudels** are always superb, as are the exotic **cakes**. Each big café seems to have its own *torte*, or cake, to compete with the ubiquitous layered chocolate *Sachertorte* of the café of the same name. The Viennese choose from some 20 different **breads** and **rolls** at breakfast, or *Frühstück* (it means 'early bit'). You can't go wrong with rye. **Cheeses** include the hard black-cased *Weinkäse*, the soft *Liptauer* spread served at Heuriger wine taverns near the Vienna Woods, and the *Kracher* with its intense aroma and ivory and emerald-green marbling.

> **Say Cheese!**
> The Viennese love their cheese. Any market will have dozens to choose from. **Steirerkas** is intense and usually crumbled over bread. **Brimsen** is a salted cream cheese made from sheep's milk. The **Liptauer** is typical of a Heuriger: cream cheese, pepper, caraway and onions. **Weinkäse**: during the six weeks this cheese has to age it is repeatedly rubbed with wine yeast. It has an almost black rind. **Kracher** is a noble rot cheese that is improved with a special wine, the so-called *Beerenauslese*. Ivory coloured with emerald green marbling, it has a very intense, unique aroma.

Below: *Viennese, like Parisians, only buy that morning's freshest breads.*

Turkish Delight
The Turkish crescent moon emblem gave it its shape and the French may have developed it into every Parisian's nibble, but it was the Viennese who invented the lovely pastry we call croissant, or in Vienna-speak, *Beugel* or *Kipferl*. The French adopted it when Empress Maria Theresia's daughter Marie Antoinette (who probably never said 'let the people eat cake') married the king of France and lost her head in the Revolution. Grünangergasse 8 in the old city is supposed to have been the place where the first croissant was baked in 1683. Look out for Vienna's historic bakeries. Their names and bakery wares are usually written in gold on black glass tablets.

Vienna likes its **meat**: pork and beef. The dishes are inevitably excellent but delicate they are not, except in the top restaurants like the Kinsky. Boar à la Asterix is a speciality during the hunting season. **Soups** are always tasty. Try the *Hühnersuppe* (chicken with noodles).

The nomenclature of dishes is often different to that in Germany. A menu is called a *Speisekarte*. A basket of rolls with your meal is always extra, but you'll only be charged for those you actually eat. A sausage, roll and mustard from a *wurst* street stand is a must. There are dozens of Chinese and Japanese restaurants, usually with fancy dragon doors and '*Running Sushi*' or '*Sushi Wong*' names. Staff in Viennese restaurants all have black leather wallets slung from their belts like sixguns and they will often scribble your bill out in front of you on a pad, asking you what you ordered. Quite a few restaurants have *grande dame* lady owners.

Irish pubs offer 'Great Australian Bite Burgers' and other delicacies, and you'll find kebab stands at every tram intersection – Persian, Indian, African, Italian, even one called Good Morning Vietnam. By the way, always ask for *Schwarz,* or black, tea, or you'll get lemon.

What to Drink

Most **wine** grown on the slopes around Vienna is Grüner Veltliner, a young white wine with a fruity bouquet, the drier the better. Then there are Rieslings from the Wachau on the Danube River hills. The red wines, the experts will tell you, have improved dramatically in recent years. Try

Blaufränkisch (Blue Frank), but not the inexpensive supermarket variety. A definite is *Most*, the juice of freshly pressed grapes prior to fermentation into wine. Or even better, *Sturm*, sold in open bottles and only available in autumn – a sort of halfway house wine. The cloudy unfiltered young *Staubiger* (dusty one) and the '*This Year's*', or *Heuriger,* are excellent. In restaurants you will often buy wine by the glass, which is equal to an eighth or quarter of a litre. A bottle of wine contains seven-eighths of a litre.

Austria is the world's fifth-largest consumer of **beer** per person. Half a pint is a *Seidl* and half a litre is a *Krügerl*. There are rare land beers from the country, *Schankbier*, or draught 12.5% *Vollbier*. Careful. And then there's the harder-hitting, amber-coloured Bock beer. *Double Bock* is strictly for mountaineers and miners. The most popular Viennese canned beer is *Ottakringer* or, in patois, *Blech* (cans from the brewery's 16th district).

Above: *Landbier is a special boutique beer brewed in the countryside.*

DO&CO Albertina

Austrian, Asian and Mediterranean food. Breakfast in the morning, snacks from 15:00–18:00. Great bar, great view. Pricey. Back of the opera. Seats 50 indoors and 60 outdoors.
✉ 1010 Wien, Albertinaplatz 1
☎ (01) 5329669
🕐 Open daily 09:00–24:00
💰 Over €25
🖳 www.doco.com

Fabio's

Fairly pricey top-notch Italian restaurant. Popular with local folk. Seats 120.
✉ 1010 Wien, Tuchlauben 4–6
☎ (01) 53222222
🕐 Mon–Sat 10:00–01:00,
💰 Over €18–25.

Harry's Time

Creative and diverse dishes. Popular with young people employed in the nearby banks and offices. Black and white décor.
✉ 1010 Wien, Dr. Karl

Lueger-Platz 5
☎ (01) 5124556
🕐 Mon–Fri 10:00–01:00, Sat 18:00–24:00
💰 €18–25

Livingstone

Great steaks and seafood. Palms, wood and colonial ambience. Food is prepared until 03:30 in the morning. Seats 130 indoors and 80 outdoors.
✉ 1010 Wien, Zelinkagasse 4
☎ (01) 5333393/15
🕐 Open daily 17:00–04:00
💰 €12–18

Mörwald im Ambassador

Expensive, famous, good classic European cuisine. Seats 80 indoors and 12 out-doors.
✉ 1010 Wien, Kärntnerstrasse 22
☎ (01) 96161161
🕐 Open daily 11:00–15:00, 18:00–23:00
💰 Over €25

Regina Margherita

Posh pizzeria in the

heart of the city. Served in a beautiful outdoor dining area in the courtyard of Palais Esterházy.
✉ 1010 Wien, Palais Esterházy, Wallnerstrasse 4
☎ (01) 5330812
🕐 Open daily 12:00–15:00 and 18:00–24:00
💰 €12–18

Sky Restaurant

Everyone's favourite view of Vienna city. Seats 200.
✉ 1010 Wien, Kärntnerstrasse 19,
☎ (01) 5131712,
🕐 Open Mon–Sat 18:00–01:00, open as a café 10:30–18:00,
💰 €18–25.

Yohm

Hip Asian restaurant with dishes from everywhere east of Kathmandu. Especially fish. Not far from Stephansdom, city centre. Seats 40.
✉ 1010 Wien, Petersplatz 3
☎ (01) 5332900
🕐 Open daily 12:00–15:00 and

Left: *Café Sperl, which opened its doors in 1880, still has its 100-year-old décor.*

18:00–24:00
🔥 *€18–25*

Zum Schwarzen Kameel

Family-run restaurant in the heart of the old city. Traditional Viennese cuisine. Also snacks. Many locals. Look for the Black Camel sign dating from 1618. Seats 75.
✉ *1010 Wien, Bognergasse 5*
☎ *(01) 5338125*
🕐 *Open Mon–Sat 08:30–24:00*
🔥 *€18–25*

Café Hummel

Watch local folk play cards, chess and bridge in this traditional café. Family run since 1937. Sitting on the terrace can be noisy. Seats 120.
✉ *1080 Wien, Josefstädterstrasse 66*
☎ *(01) 4055314*
🕐 *Open Mon–Sat 07:00–24:00*
🔥 *€12–18*

Café Landtmann

Elegant coffee house near the Burgtheater, founded 1873. All the traditional Viennese coffee specialities and dishes. Sigmund Freud, Marlene Dietrich and Paul McCartney have all eaten here. Seats 380 indoors and 350 outdoors.
✉ *1010 Wien, Dr. Karl Lueger-Ring*
☎ *(01) 241000*
🕐 *Open daily 07:30–24:00*
🔥 *€12–18*

Classy *Kaffeehaus*
Coffee houses are synonymous with Vienna.
Café Central: 1, Herrengasse 14. Where poets, writers and litterati argued at the turn of the 19th century. Neo-Gothic vaulting, tuxedoed waiters.
Café Sperl: 6, Gumpendorfer Strasse 11. Every film maker's choice of café. Original décor; Hitler's favourite.
Café Weimar: 9, Währingerstrasse 68. A corner café with cosy booths and strawberry cakes in season.
Café Demel: 1, Kohlmarkt. Demel, a 200-year-old café, is one of two cafés that claim to have the original Sachertorte recipe.
Café Landtman: 1, Dr-Karl-Lueger-Ring 4. Ideally located on the Ringstrasse.
There are some 80 grand old cafés in Vienna. Be prepared for the occasional head waiter snootiness, an act they reserve, tongue-in-cheek, for new customers, to maintain tradition.

EF16

New restaurant under 400-year-old arches. Northern Italian 'Osteria' style. Mixture of Italian and Viennese specialities. Seats 60.

✉ 1010 Wien, Fleischmarkt 16
☎ (01) 5132318
🕓 Open Mon–Fri 11:30–15:00, Mon–Sat 17:30–23:00
💰 €12–18

Gastwirtschaft Huth

A 'noble' Viennese *Beisl* serving traditional as well as creative new Viennese cuisine. Seats 60.

Below: *Sachertorte, the quintessential and world-famous Viennese chocolate cake.*

✉ 1010 Wien, Schellinggasse 5
☎ (01) 5135644
🕓 Open daily 11:30–24:00
💰 €12–17

Lusthaus

Surrounded by the Prater (huge recreational area across the Danube). Very romantic. Nice terrace.

✉ 1020 Wien, Freudenau 254 (at the end of Prater Hauptallee)
☎ (01) 7289565
🕓 Open May–Sep: Thu–Tue 12:00–23:00, Sat–Sun 12:00–18:00, Wed closed. Open Oct–Apr daily 12:00–18:00.
💰 €12–18

Más

Trendy. Lots of young locals. Cocktail bar, good Latin-American dishes. Have some tapas. Seats 120.

✉ 1080 Wien, Laudongasse 36
☎ (01) 4038324
🕓 Mon–Wed and Sun 18:00–24:00, Thu–Sat 18:00–01:00
💰 €12–18

Meixner's Gastwirtschaft

Classic Viennese cuisine with seasonal specialities. Beautiful garden. Seats 120 indoors and 45 outdoors.

✉ 1100 Wien, Buchengasse 64
☎ (01) 6042710
🕐 Open daily 11:30–22:00
💰 €12–18

Naschmarkt

Tiny restaurants: traditional Austrian cuisine, also food from the Balkans and Far East. There is anything from Palatschinken to seafood, kebab and wok. Multicultural melting pot Vienna – the city's most lively market.

🚇 U4 station Karlsplatz or Kettenbrückengasse
🕐 Open 06:00–22:00
💰 €2–15

Palmenhaus im Burggarten

Restaurant in a Victorian station-like palm house. A former botanical garden. Few but creative dishes. Outdoor terrace. Tropical butterfly house next door. Seats 130 indoors and 250 outdoors.

✉ 1010 Wien, Burggarten (entrance at the Albertina)
☎ (01) 5331033
🕐 Open daily 10:00–02:00
💰 €12–18

Wolf

Combination of a traditional Viennese Beisl (pub) and a trendy, modern restaurant. Marvellous 'new' Viennese cuisine, fine selection of wines.

✉ 1070 Wien, Burggasse 76
☎ (01) 9906620
💰 €12–18

Zur Alten Kaisermühle

Right on the Danube before Kagraner Bridge. Seats 120.

✉ 1220 Wien, Fischerstrand 21A
☎ (01) 2633529
🕐 Open daily 11:30–23:00
💰 €12–18

Beim Cumpelik

Friendly, rustic Beisl in the centre of a Biedermeier neighbourhood in the 8th district. Traditional Viennese cuisine. Seats 75.

✉ 1080 Wien, Buchfeldgasse 10
☎ (01) 4032520
🕐 Open Mon–Sat 11:00–14:30, 17:30–23:00
💰 €8–12

Blaustern

Nice café and restaurant, popular with students from the nearby university. Good breakfasts. Seats 130 indoors and 90 outdoors.

✉ 1190 Wien, Döblinger Gürtel 2
☎ (01) 3696564
🕐 Open Mon–Fri 07:00–01:00, Sat–Sun 08:00–02:00
💰 €8–12

Brückenwirt

Rustic, friendly pub on the outskirts of Vienna. Traditional Viennese cuisine in huge portions.

✉ 1100 Wien,

Unterlaaerstrasse 27
☎ (01) 6883883
💰 €12 and under

Café Stein

Famous Viennese café close to the old university on the Ringstrasse. Cosy ambience.
✉ 1090 Wien, Währingerstrasse 6–8
☎ (01) 3197241
🕐 Open Mon–Sat 07:00–01:00
💰 €8–12

Centimeter I

Concentric restaurant chain; order sandwiches by centimetres. There is a huge variety of beers. Groups can choose one huge shared dish. Wheelbarrow or Sword are favourites. Haunt of young Viennese. Seats 120.
✉ 1080 Wien, Lenaugasse 11
☎ (01) 470060641
🕐 Open Mon–Fri 10:00–24:00, Sat–Sun 11:00–01:00
💰 €6–8

Glacisbeisl

Trendily designed Beisl inside Museums Quartier. Traditional Viennese cuisine with a modern interpretation.
✉ 1070 Wien, Museums Quartier, Zugang Breitegasse 4
☎ (01) 5265660
🕐 Open daily 11:00–02:00
💰 €8–12

Kopp

Traditional Viennese cuisine, huge portions, reasonable prices. Seats 100.
✉ 1200 Wien, Donaueschingen-strasse 28
☎ (01) 3328082
🕐 Open daily 06:00–02:00
💰 €15 and under

Plachutta Hietzing

The restaurants of the Plachutta family (there is also one in the 1st district and one in the 19th) are famous for their Viennese beef dishes. Be sure to taste the Tafelspitz boiled fillet of beef.
✉ 1130 Wien, Auhofstrasse 1
☎ (01) 8777087
💰 €15 and under

Nells Gastwirtschaft

Between Währing and Gertshof districts in the western suburbs. Seats 130 indoors and 80 outdoors.
✉ 1180 Wien, Alseggerstrasse 26
☎ (01) 4791377
💰 €8–12

Oktagon

Remote Wienerwald, ideal place to relax after a walk in the Vienna Woods. Incredible views over Vienna. Ask for the poppy seed cake.
✉ 1190 Wien, Himmelstrasse Ecke Höhenstrasse
☎ (01) 3288936
🕐 Open Wed–Fri 12:00–22:00, Sat–Sun 11:00–22:00
💰 €12 and under

Rudi's Beisl

Tiny little Beisl serving Viennese cuisine at its best. Reservation required. Seats 30.
✉ 1050 Wien, Wiedner Hauptstrasse 88
☎ (01) 5445102
🕐 Open Mon–Fri 11:00–15:00,

18:00–23:00

💰 *€15 and under*

Salettl Pavillon

Frequented mostly by locals from the surrounding area. Very romantic. Try the ham-and-cheese croissant. Seats 50 indoors and 250 outdoors.

✉ *1190 Wien, Hartäckerstrasse 80*

☎ *(01) 4792222*

🕐 *Open daily 06:30–01:00*

💰 *€8–12*

Wrenkh

Tiny restaurant in the city centre. Specializes in vegetarian dishes but also meat and fish. The organic fruit juices are freshly prepared.

✉ *1010 Wien, Bauernmarkt 10*

☎ *(01) 5331526*

🕐 *Open Mon–Sat 11:30–23:00*

💰 *€8–12*

Zu den 2 Lieserln

Actually a sight in itself. The Viennese have been eating schnitzel and roasts here since the days of Marshal Radetzky, who crushed the 1848 revolution. Try the onion and vanilla roast.

✉ *1070 Wien, Burggasse 63*

☎ *(01) 5233282*

🕐 *Open daily 11:00–23:00*

💰 *€8–12*

Weingut Mayer on Pfarrplatz

Heuriger wine farm, inner courtyard, not far from Grinzing in an old farmhouse where Beethoven once lived. The new wine is the one to taste e.g. Grüner Veltliner. Seats 200.

✉ *Pfarrplatz 2*

☎ *(01) 3703361*

🕐 *Open daily 16:00–24:00 except Sun 11:00–24:00*

💰 *€12–18*

Die Wirtschaft

Viennese pub and garden, personally run by owner Bouka Bank who also has a restaurant in the Vienna Woods. Take Tram 41 to the end of the line. Seats 80.

✉ *Pötzleinsdorfer-strasse 67*

☎ *(01) 4792857*

🕐 *Open daily except Sun and Mon 11:00–24:00*

💰 *€12 and under*

Ilona Stuberl

Small Hungarian restaurant off the Graben. Try the prune soup with almonds, and fried carp. Seats 50.

✉ *Bräunerstrasse 2, Innere Stadt*

☎ *(01) 5339029*

🕐 *Open daily 11:30–23:30 Apr–Sep. Rest of year closed on Mon,*

💰 *€12–18*

Café Central

You wait at the door, a smart, jacketed waiter will take your coat. World newspapers are available to read all day. The ceiling is neo-Gothic and a pianist plays light music. Trotsky was a regular here. Seats 150.

✉ *Herrengasse 14*

☎ *(01) 5336763*

🕐 *Open 07:30–22:00 and Sun 10:00–18:00*

💰 *A coffee costs €3.50*

ENTERTAINMENT
Nightlife

Vienna has an extraordinary range of entertainment for a relatively small city, from the sublime Musikverein, Staatsoper, Johann Strauss Capelle, Spanish Riding School and Vienna Boys' Choir to the more avant-garde desires at the other end of the taste spectrum. Latest events can be found in *Listings*, a German weekly but easy to decipher. You can buy them at lamp post slots. Vienna is not really an all-night hip-hop town so expect some earlier than usual closing times.

Opera

The Vienna State Opera (Staatsoper) and the less formal Volksoper are often the reason that many come to Vienna. The Opera House, when it was opened in 1869 as the first grand building of the emperor's Ringstrasse project, was not particularly impressive. The Kaiser said so, too. Consequently Edward Van der Null, co-architect, hung himself. The Volks-oper in Währingerstrasse is less expensive and specializes in lighter all-join-in operetta. Tickets vary from €10 to €250. The Staats-oper, Volksoper, Academietheater, Burgtheater and Schauspielhaus share a common box office: Bundestheaterkassen, ⊠ 1 Hanuschgasse 3, ☎ 514447780, 🚇 Karlsplatz, 🖳 www.bundestheater.at

Music

Vienna is probably the most musical city in the world – much of Western classical music developed here. Mozart, Schubert, Bruckner, Schönberg, Beethoven, Brahms – the list is endless. The Vienna Philharmonic Orchestra is possibly the world's best (a moveable accolade), the Vienna Symphony not far behind. The Vienna Boys' Choir have performed in the same royal chapel for 500 years. In Vienna you can see collections of ancient Stradivarius violins and visit the graves of famous composers.

There are at least 30 musical venues, and dozens of churches offering music, with Gregorian chant a speciality. Vienna has always been a world-renowned centre of Western classical music and opera. Franz Schubert, Brahms, Brückner, Josef Haydn, Mozart, Beethoven and Mahler spent long periods composing and playing in Vienna. Classical music resonates in Western man's

Opposite: *A Danube boat cruise by night.*
Left: *Vienna's State Opera House facing frantic Opernring Street. Pavarotti and all the greats of the European opera world have sung here.*

consciousness. We may not recognize the piece of music, but somehow we can hum the tune.

There is a long tradition in Vienna of *Strassenmusik* (street music). This is not at all like busking on the London Underground. You will see a student playing the cello in a Hofburg portal, or another, with her own backing on tape, singing opera. An elderly man in an Alpine hat and tweed overcoat plays a violin, a jolly fellow in Am Hof market, a trumpet. They pop up everywhere. After all, this is the City of Music. And they are very good. Be generous: one of them may become a Strauss or Mozart one day.

Theatre

There are 16 theatres in Vienna with the **Volksoper**, **Burgtheater** and **Volkstheater** probably the most popular and the **English Theatre** offering regular performances. The Theatre of the Imperial Court, or Burgtheater,

Right: *Originally known as the Theatre of the Imperial Court, the Burg Theatre is one of the oldest play-houses in Europe.*

Left: The Volkstheater, or People's Theatre, looks over the busy Museums Quartier.

is a curved, bulbous building opened in 1888, the premier classic theatre of the German-speaking world at the time. Today it concentrates on Shakespeare and 'serious' theatre.

Visibility used to be poor, acoustics worse and the Viennese would say: 'In the Rathaus you see nothing, in Parliament you hear nothing (not much democratic debate was allowed), while in the Burgtheater you neither see nor hear.' It has improved considerably since then. It seats 1300 people, facing sumptuous boxes, galleries, frescoes, and, not terribly imaginatively, a picture frame stage. The grand, claret-carpeted staircases in each wing, flanked by candelabras and busts of playrights, sweep up to a 60m (200ft) curved foyer. Post performance, you can enjoy a coffee at the nearby Café Landtmann. Vienna's Sigmund Freud certainly did, usually with one of their famous Guglhupf cakes.

Royalty had its Burg, or royal, theatre so naturally the people had to have a Volks-theater.

Vienna's Shakespeare

There is a square and an underground station named after Johann Nepomuk Nestroy. Born in 1801, he wrote 83 plays and was famous for his mastery of the Viennese dialect, folk tradition and Viennese popular theatre. He also had an acerbic wit and often had to skirt around the censors and all-powerful Minister Metternich to get parody and criticism on stage, always veiling it with comedy.

Right: Sorrow and symphony are reflected in the eyes of this Viennese street violinist.

Bells of St Stephen's

Europe's second largest church bell, after the one in Cologne Cathedral, is housed in the North Tower of Stephansdom. It is known, from its rich resonant clang, as the *Pummerin*, or Boomer. The first *Pummerin* weighing 22,500kg (49,613lb) and cast from Turkish cannonballs in 1711, was destroyed in the World War II fire that ravaged the cathedral. The new bell, hoisted in 1957, weighs a mere 21,383kg (47,150lb) and is decorated with Turkish siege and 1945 fire scenes. Part of the inscription reads, 'Burst apart in the white heat of conflagration, I fell as the city moaned under the burden of war and fear'. Stephansdom has a total of 11 bells, including the *Half-Pummerin*, the *Feuerin*, (fire alarm bell), the *Kantnerin*, *Fehringerin* and *Bieringerin* – the latter rung 250 years ago to tell all the pubs in the vicinity 'Time, gentlemen, please. Last round.'

Bohemian Folk

Walk up the side of the theatre on Burggasse for 50m (55 yds) – mind the traffic. On the corner of Breitegasse there is a huge old fob watch hanging above the corner, supposedly the smallest house in Vienna and home to watchmaker Friedrich Schmollgruber. It was built 130 years ago, in 1872.

The historic cobbled Spittelberg pedestrian area a little further, on the right of Burggasse, has always been a Bohemian area of old houses, actors, artists, restaurants, craft shops and boutiques. It was a workers' area and at one time Vienna's Red Light district.

Painting the Town

The clubbing scene is not vast in Vienna, but it is intimate with good jazz bars and lots of Austro-pop. All places are reasonably priced (maximum €20). Vienna is far from being old-fashioned, however. There are 50 rock and pop gigs weekly, and plenty of café concerts. In effect, music is around every corner, even if it is only a street busker's divine cello.

Cinema

Vienna's excellent International Film Festival, the Viennale, takes place in October. Most films shown in Vienna are in German but check in the newspapers, *Der Standard* or *Die Presse*, for listings in English. 'OF' means that the film is in the original, and 'OmeU' means it has English subtitles. Arts International in the Innere Stadt shows English films, as does the English Cinema. The Bellaria specializes in old black-and-white Austrian-German movies, while the Burg Kino regularly features *The Third Man* in its original English. There is cinema under the stars in the Augarten, July–August. *Bride of the Wind*, a film on Gustav Mahler's wife Alma, is intriguing. *The Piano Teacher*, based on Elfriede Jelinek's novel, won three prizes at Cannes.

Open-air Cinemas
Films in English are often shown at the *Kino Unter Sternen*, Cinema Under the Stars, below the Flaktürme in lovely Augarten Park – where the porcelain is made. ◷ mid-Jul to mid-Aug. There are seven such open-air cinemas in Vienna, with great eats, new friends, great fun.

Left: *Young men dressed as 18th-century courtiers encourage visitors to attend concert performances.*

Right: *The Spring Festival generally runs from the end of March to the beginning of April.*

Cool Vienna

Downtown sound, techno beats – Vienna is not only Mozart, opera and classical orchestras – there is plenty of Austro-pop for the young folk. Rock star Christina Stümer was born in 1982. Her first hit was *Ich Liebe*, and then an anti-Iraq war song called *Mama ana Ahabak*. Next came *Vorbei*. Her 2005 album *Schwarz Weiss* reached number three on the German album charts. In 2006, she sold 1.5 million discs. Other Austro-pop artists include: Rainhard Fendrich (he sings in Viennese dialect), Georg Danzer, who died in 2007, and Wolfgang Ambros whose *Schifoan* is practically the anthem of skiers. Top of the pops was Falco, who died in a car accident 10 years ago.

Festivals

Fasching

No mere carnival or Mardi Gras, Vienna's dance (*Fasching*) starts with balls on 11 November and goes right through until Ash Wednesday, usually at weekends. So who said the Viennese were staid? In fact, Vienna always had a reputation during Habsburg times as being something of a wild spot – the waltz was seriously groovy in its heyday. There are some 300 balls in all, ranging from masked *Gschnas* wonders to a sort of (to the sophisticates of Vienna) country hick *Burgenländischen Kroaten*. To learn all about it and where to learn the tango and foxtrot, 🖳 www.ball.at

Frühlingsfestival

In spring, classical concerts are all the buzz.
🕓 March to early April.

International Accordion Festival

The accordion is a favourite instrument of Austria and much of the Balkans.
🕓 End of February through March.

Danube Island Festival

Pop, folk, country, rock and everything in-between. It attracts up to 3 million tourists and it's all free.
🕓 Late June on a three-day weekend.

Visual Arts

Architecture:
Architektur Zentrum Wein, ✉ Museums Quartier.

Photography:
Westlicht, ✉ 7, Westbahnstrasse 40.

Contemporary Sculpture:
Generali Foundation, ✉ 4, Wiedner Hauptstrasse 15.

Contemporary Art:
Kunsthalle Wien, ✉ Museumsplatz 1.

Left: *Accordion music is very popular in Austria.*

Right: *The Old Baths in Baden were built 100 years ago in the Renaissance style. They are equipped today with the most modern technology, and attract visitors to come again and again.*

BADEN

Baden may seem reserved but it has 'a past'. It was the setting for the 1870s novel *Venus im Pelze*, translated as *Venus in Fur*, by **Count Sacher-Masoch**, whose deviancy gave birth to the expression 'sadomasochism', a play on his name.

Up into the park, past avenues of trees, is a monument to the **Strauss** family surrounded in spring by banks of red tulips. The higher up the path you climb the better the view of both the spa and Baden.

If you would like to take the waters, try the **Thermalstrandbad** on Helenenstrasse or the indoor **Römertherme**. **Doblhoffpark** nearby has formal gardens, an Orangerie and woods. Not far from Baden is **Gumpolds-kirchen**, a wine-growing area full of folksy Heurigen drinking spots.

The S-Bahn from Vienna's Südbahnhof station gets you to Baden.

Baden Museums
The **Rollett Museum**, south of the Schwechat on Weikersdorfplatz, is a fanciful 1905 Neo-Renaissance building housing a collection of death masks, skulls and 'arcanobilia'. The **Franz Josef Museum** has arms, military uniforms, banknotes, penny-farthing bicycles and just about anything the local folk have managed to collect.

BUDAPEST

Life is more hectic in poorer Budapest than in Vienna: the traffic, the people, the gypsy music, the noise and the rather frenetic rush for business. Possibly the best way to see the city on a short visit is to take a 'Go Local' tour of four to five people led by 'Underguides' who speak a dozen languages.

Hungary converted to Christianity 1000 years ago. The land was invaded by Mongols in the 13th century. The Magyar people mixed with the Slavs, Moravians, Germans, and Turks. From all this emerged a colourful, dynamic and at times warlike people, but above all a fascinating culture, much of which can be seen on Budapest's skyline ridge overlooking the Danube – a series of castles and churches and historical treasures.

The Hungarian people rose up against Soviet dictatorship in 1956, but in spite of bloody fighting in the streets with students jumping onto Russian tanks to hurl Molotov cocktails down the hatches, the revolt was brutally put down and former premier Imre Nagy executed. It would not be until 1991, after the Berlin wall was breached and the Soviet Union collapsed, that Hungary would at last be free of Communist domination.

> **Budapest's Bridges**
> The old green-girded Szabadság bridge, built in 1896, has been closed for anti-corrosion work costing €19 million. But there are five others spanning the Danube between Buda and Pest: the white, clean structure of the Elizabeth Bridge over the narrowest part of the Danube, and the *Széchenyi lánchid* (Széchenyi Chain Bridge) are two. The latter was built in 1849, the city's first permanent bridge. The chains but not the pillars were destroyed in both World Wars.

Left: *Széchenyi Chain Bridge across the Danube, looking towards Budapest's Royal Palace.*

On the outskirts of the Danube-divided capital of Buda and Pest (which is pronounced Pesht) is the red wall-surrounded Statue Park, a circular open museum of the former communist public statues in Budapest. Soviet 'Baroque' is remarkable for its propaganda, naivety, sentimentality and, above all, size. Comrade Lenin is here, hand outstretched, guiding the world forward to scientific socialism.

THE BLUE DANUBE

A river cruise along the beautiful Danube, especially the Wachau valley, is an excellent excursion from Vienna. For full details, *see* Highlights, pages 32–33.

KREMS AND DÜRNSTEIN

Charted in the 12th century, Krems is located at the confluence of the Danube and Krems rivers, 88km (55 miles) northwest of Vienna. For more details, *see* Highlights, pages 32–33.

Nine kilometres (5.6 miles) upriver from Krems is Dürnstein. For two years (1192–94)

Right: *Dürnstein castle and village on the Danube.*

Richard the Lionheart was held captive in Dürnstein until the huge ransom Emperor Henry VI demanded was paid. Richard eventually bought his freedom, partly through taxation in England. The ruins of the castle are on a hill directly above Dürnstein. Its baby-blue and white Baroque **church tower** stands on the riverside on ramparts that look as if they have been there since Richard the Lionheart was forced to disembark.

As the Danube twists and turns between the hills, the river bank opens to reveal rolling slopes of vines and two red-capped old churches: **Weissenkirchen** (the white church), and the **late Gothic church** in the village of Spitz, which also has a navigation museum and some fabulous wines.

In the forested area that comes up next, the 'Venus of Willendorf' was excavated. This 25,000-year-old **fertility statuette**, possibly the oldest (and ugliest) piece of European art carved out of limestone, is now in the prehistoric section of the **Natural History Museum** in Vienna.

MELK

The giant mustard yellow Melk Benedictine Abbey, first built in 1089, stands high above the Danube and the tiny village that grew at its feet in medieval times. As you look directly up from the little streets of the village with their ancient historical wall plaques, the façade of the abbey stretches for 1115m (3695ft).

Dominating the river from every direction, Melk was a Roman 'Limes' or border post 2000 years ago before becoming a pre-Habsburg dynasty Babenberg fortress

> **Smoking in Vienna**
> 'Smoking can kill you.' *'Rauchen kann tödlich sein.'* This warning is displayed on every packet of cigarettes in the world, but Vienna is reasonably smoking-friendly. All hotels have smoking and non-smoking rooms. There are no restaurants or cafés where you cannot smoke, albeit nearly all will have carefully demarcated areas. There are many tiny *Tabak* shops on almost every corner. In Vienna's Tobacco Museum, you can browse through 2500 objects and learn about nicotine and its history since the Spanish and Portuguese adventurers first brought the weed to Europe 500 years ago. To stamp out a cigar, incidentally, is not done. Let it die of its own accord.

Above: *Melk Monastery's mustard exterior contains a wealth of Baroque art.*

and, in 1089, an abbey. The present abbey was built in the early 18th century by local builder Jakob Prandtauer.

The church's interior was decorated by itinerant Italian masters whose fund of imaginative design was obviously unlimited. Rolling wave-topped marble columns, roof roundels and thousands of colourful frescoes adorn every bit of the ceiling. There are balustrades and clouds and angels on the pulpit and on the scrolls of the organ gallery. The walls seem to shiver, blazon, and ripple as if revelling in the vast lashings of gilt.

There is nothing real about it at all. It is not meant to be. The idea was to give the congregation an ethereal glimpse of the joys of paradise. The display of wealth, power, art, pomp and glory takes your breath away, and that of the half-million visitors who come here each year. Spirituality is left to a small

MELK

'**Silent Room**' to the side of the main church with its one candle, one Joseph lily in a glass vase and its unadorned simplicity. Melk is a Slavic word meaning 'slow-moving stream'.

The monastery's long, many-sectioned **museum** includes an 11th-century portable altar made of walrus horn, and fascinating religious art of the later Middle Ages. Most of **St Koloman's body** lies in Melk Abbey while his head lies in Hungary. He was formerly **Austria's patron saint**, only to be deposed by St Leopold. Melk was occupied on two occasions by the French during the Napoleonic wars. It was a Nazi secondary school in World War II.

The grand **Marble Hall** is linked to the **Library** by an open balcony with expansive views of Melk, the Danube and surrounding hills. Both Library and Marble Hall have huge and magnificent ceiling frescoes by Paul Troger (1731–32). There are some 16,000 leather-bound books here, a total of 100,000 in the monastery, including 750 *incunabula*, or books made prior to the invention of the printing press. The oldest goes back to the 9th century.

The quiet monastery **gardens**, **Stiftspark**, are a joy to walk through. There is a lovely **open-air restaurant** near the entrance. There is also a **café** in the Baroque **Garten-pavillon** with incredible frescoes of Western adventurers and lovely ladies meeting up under giggle conditions with the natives and animals of India, as well as Africa and the Far East.

The town of Melk itself, with its turreted houses, cute painted shutters, tiny lanes and family shops, is a delight to stroll through, or just sit and observe.

Old Melk Tavern
You'll see a narrow cobbled lane, a restaurant jutting out over the tops of houses below, flowers and a creeper-covered patio. Right below the rock face that soars upward to the walls of Melk Monastery, the Goldener Stern tavern (built in AD1500) transports you back in time. The houses to the left and right announce proudly that one was built in 1390 and another, quotes a writer, in 1230. Two thousand years ago, the Romans built a fort not far from here towards the river which they called Namare.

Right: *A typical tram stop sign.*

High Season and Holidays
1 Jan • New Year
6 Jan • Epiphany
Easter Monday • major holiday weekend
1 May • Labour day
6th Thursday after Easter • Ascension Day
6th Monday after Easter • Whit Monday
2nd Thursday after Whitsuntide • Corpus Christi
15 August • Assumption Day
1 November • All Saints' Day (thousands visit cemeteries)
26 October • Austria National Day
25 December • Christmas Day, *Weihnachtstag*
26 December • Boxing Day or St Stephen's Day

Tourist Information

Austrian Tourist Office: They have a range of brochures and information on any query.
✉ Margaretenstrasse 1
🚇 U4 to Margaretengürtel, ☎ (01) 588 660 or 0810 101818,
💻 www.austria.info
Closed at weekends.

Vienna Tourist Office: Not as good or multilingual as the above.
✉ 1 Albertinaplatz/Maysedergasse
☎ (01) 24555
🚇 Karlsplatz
💻 www.vienna.info
🕘 Open 09:00–19:00 daily.

General Information

For booking hotels, car rental, etc.
💻 www.tiscover.com

Entry Requirements

EU citizens require only a valid national identity card. Everyone else (including UK visitors) needs a passport. No visas needed for Australian, British Canadian, New Zealand and US citizens. South Africans require a visa.

Customs

Bring in as much as you like if the items were purchased in another EU country. But if you are coming from a non-EU country or the goods were purchased in a dutyfree store, much lower limits apply, e.g. 200 cigarettes, one litre of spirits. Uncooked meat, weapons, drugs, dairy products, animal skins, and so on may get you into trouble with the customs officers.

Health

There are no special requirements for entry into Vienna unless you are coming from endemic disease areas (check with your travel agent or nearest Austrian embassy). Austria has a superb health care system. Having an EU or British passport ensures free health care. Take out medical insurance, however; the free health variety involves much filling in of forms. Serious ill-nesses will always be treated quickly and money concerns discussed later.

What to Pack

Vienna can be very hot in summer and very cold with an icy wind in winter. You can buy anything locally, of course, but shorts, sandals, sun cream, shades and hat

for summer are advisable. Summer is also the highest rainfall season, so bring an umbrella. A good pair of walking boots will be useful for the many parks and Vienna Woods. Bring jacket and tie for the opera. For winter visitors, dress as you would for any country where it snows. A Swiss knife (in hold luggage) is always handy. And a novel.

Money Matters

Currency:
Euro banknotes come in the following denominations: 5, 10, 20, 50, 100, 200 and 500. Always carry a 50 cent coin on you for the WC. Banks are open ☼ 08:00–12:30 and 13:30–15:00.

Exchange Rates:
The Euro is stable and does not change much. Roughly €1.50 to the UK pound and €0.75 to the US dollar. Travellers' cheques are not as useful as ATM credit cards.

Spaced Out
In April 2007, Kàroly Simonyi – who took American citizenship in the 1980s – became the second Hungarian to travel in space. And for speaking Hungarian in space, Kàroly was presented with the Hungarian Cross of Merit. The billionaire Microsoft developer spent a fortnight on board the International Space Station 380km (236 miles) above earth. It cost him US$25 million. In 1980 Bertalan Farkas, another Hungarian, spent a week in space with a Soviet cosmonaut.

Wechselstube, or exchange booths, that accept major currencies are available in the city.

ATMs and Credit Cards:

Widely available and widely used. Credit cards are not as widely used (in shops and restaurants) as, e.g., in the UK and USA.

Accommodation

Reserve your hotel (on the web) before you arrive, at least for the first three nights. There is every type of hotel, wine farm, apartment and backpacker's lodge available. Hotels will often negotiate if you are staying a while but not necessarily in the high summer season. A continental breakfast usually comes with the room.

Eating Out

Eating out is the Vienna thing to do. There are some 2000 restaurants, cafés, pubs and bars. Apart from Viennese specialities (especially coffee and cakes and 'slices', or *schnitzels*), there are Japanese, Chinese (lots), Indian, Thai, Greek, Italian (lots), Balkan, American (burgers), French, Israeli, Hungarian, Russian, Tibetan, Brazilian, Levantine, and Korean places – the lot. No need to dress up but in the smarter restaurants you will feel out of place in trainers and T-shirt. Vienna's cuisine concentrates on meats (try boar), but fish from the Danube is good. And you must try a fast-food *wurst* (sausage), mustard and roll at any of a hundred corner stands.

Business Hours

All shops, except bakeries, are closed on Sundays. And many smaller ones close for lunch. Hours are: ⊕ 08:00 or 09:00 to about 18:00.

Some museums stay open with free entrance. School summer holidays are in July–August. Quite a few galleries and theatres close for part of the time, otherwise they are open Tuesday–Sunday, ⊕ 10:00–18:00. Churches (many with fabulous interiors) are open ⊕ 07:00–19:00 but in quite a few you can only get into the grilled foyer.

Time

Vienna time is GMT plus one hour in summer and plus two hours in winter.

Communications

Telephones: The international dialling code for Vienna is ☎ +431 or 00431. Phone booths have instructions in four languages. Note: for numbers ending in 0, no need to dial the final 0. This final 0 means it's a line with direct dial extensions. Phone cards are more common than cash at booths. Buy them at any Tabak, Trafik or post office. A telephone charge card from home, using a pin number, is convenient.

Directory enquiries: ☎ 118877. *Mobile*: ☎ 0800 664 664.

Mobiles: Known as 'Handy' in Vienna. Everyone seems to have one and to spend a good deal of time thereon. Check with your mobile service provider before leaving home to see if your package will function in Vienna – unless you have a tri-band phone.

Internet Cafés: There are plenty. In addition, restaurants and cafés – in keeping with the Viennese tradition of free newspaper reading – will allow you access. The AOL access number from Vienna is ☎ 585 8483, Compuserve is 0049-180 570 40 70, and EUnet is 899 330.

Post: Look up *Post und Telegraphenverwaltung* for the post office nearest to you. The postal service is excellent, staff usually are English-speaking. There are post offices at the three main railway stations. The main post office is at ✉ 1 Fleischmarkt, not far from Schwedenplatz, 🚇 U-Bahn U1 or U4. ⏰ Open daily from 06:00–22:00.

Electricity

220V – quite acceptable for, e.g., British 240V appliances. Bring an adaptor (plugs have 2 pins) and transformer if you have 110V equipment.

Weights and Measures

Vienna uses the metric system.

Health Precautions

Most visitors drink water in blue bottles but the Vienna tap water is perfectly safe and tasty. Vienna is a café culture society, so tainted food is exceptionally rare. If you get travel diarrhoea, the nearest Apotheke will advise you to drink diluted cola and eat as little as possible.

Useful Phrases

Good day • *Grüss Gott*
(*Guten tag* is more German)
Please • *Bitte*
Thank you • *Danke* (in Vienna pronounced *Dankeh*)
Yes • *Ja*
No • *Nein*
I don't understand • *Ich verstehe nicht*
Where is …? • *Wo ist?*
Do you speak English? • *Sprechen Sie Englisch?*
Left • *Links*
Right • *Rechts*
Tomorrow • *Morgen*
Entrance • *Eingang*
Tram • *Strassenbahn*
Station • *Bahnhof*
City District • *Bezirk*
Church • *Kirche*
Art • *Kunst*
Castle • *Schloss* or *Burg*
Airport • *Flughafen*
Departure • *Abfahrt*
Ticket Office • *Kasse*
Push • *Drücken*
Pull • *Ziehen*
Danger • *Gefahr*
Out of Order • *Ausser Betrieb*
Two • *Zwei*
Strawberries • *Erdbeeren*
Red Wine • *Rotwein*
White Wine • *Weisswein*
Beef • *Rindfleisch*
Sausage Kiosk • *Würstelstand*

Nothing for Me?

Some of the yellow postboxes in Austria have the following words written on them: *Haben Sie nichts für mich*? 'Haven't you got anything for me?' Three hundred years ago things were different. In Vienna, for example, mail was delivered six times a day, but the postman ran (rather than walking or going by bicycle or van) through the city, shaking a rattle to tell folk he was coming. He carried a numbered lead box with the mail inside. There were no proper postage stamps at the time – that had to wait until 1840 for Britain's adhesive Penny Black – so the receiver of the letter paid for its delivery.

Take out medical cover insurance. Pharmacies usually require a doctor's prescription. If you want to be 100% reassured, contact Medical Advisory Service to Travellers Abroad 🖳 www.masta.org

Medical Emergencies

Ambulance ☎ 144
Auto Accident ☎ 120
Vienna Medical Association Service (foreign patients), ✉ 1, Weihburggasse 10–12, ☎ 5150 1213 or 24/7 hotline 5139595, 🚇 U3, U1 Stephansplatz. The actual office is manned and open ⏲ 08:00–16:00 Mon–Wed and 08:00–18:00 Thu, and 08:00–14:00 Fri. Aids testing in Vienna can be done at AIDS-Hilfe Wien, ✉ 6, Mariahilfer Gürtel 4, 🚇 U6 Gumpendorfer, ☎ 599370.
Children's Hospital (Sankt Anna Kinderspital), ✉ 9, Kinderspitalgasse 6,

☎ 401700, 🚇 U6 Alser Strasse. Doctors are on duty 24 hours a day.
Emergency Ward Hospital Allgemeines Krankenhaus (AKH), largest hospital in Europe ✉ 9, Wärhinger Gürtel 18–20, ☎ 40 400-0.
Alcoholics Anonymous ☎ 799 5599

Note: For visitors who have been to India, Africa or South America, this may sound paranoid. But in the Vienna Woods you should be wary of ticks which can, rarely, cause Central European encephalitis (CEE). Dress as you would in Africa, in hat, long trousers and long-sleeved shirt. Pull the tick off but if itchiness or fever results, see a doctor.

Personal Safety

The only problem you may meet is a skateboarder narrowly missing you on the steps of either the Burgtheater or Belvedere Palace.

Vienna is a particularly safe city and the Viennese are famously law-abiding. The Gürtel ring roads are reputedly a trifle red-lightish and the Karlsplatz underground station a bit of a dope and punch-up booze area. Südbahnhof and Stadtpark should perhaps be avoided after dark, and Schweden-platz can be hectic. Wearing a money belt pouch immediately identifies you as a for-eigner anywhere in the world – but it is highly unlikely you'll meet a bag-snatcher. Carry a photocopy of your I.D. or passport with you. The police are armed but seldom use their weapons – yet they love racing, TV-style, sirens blazing, through the city. You will very seldom see anyone get angry: it's not the Viennese thing to do.

Useful Phrases

Actually they are not that useful as you are likely to get out of your depth if some-one thinks you speak German. However, they do break the ice (*see panel, page 87*). Rather get a small pocket dictionary which you can use to identify individual words on shops and notices and street signs. Guess the rest.

Road signs

The usual international road signs are used in Vienna. The round-city motorways are hectic. Be more care-ful at no-lights zebra crossings, especially of cars turning corners (they usually do so before you are very far into the crossing, which is allowed). But you will find that Vienna is pedestrian-friendly and the driv-ing non-aggressive.

Etiquette

Always try to speak a few (humble) words of German. Vienna is not a big city but it is one with a proud his-tory. The Viennese have a reputation for being reserved, but that soon melts into smiles and helpful-ness. The Viennese know well that tourists are important to them. Headwaiters can be stiff-lipped – but that's a traditional act. There is no need to push or shove any-where. You can wear what you like but be reasonably dress-respectful in churches (there are no decency guardians as in Rome), remembering that the Viennese are more Catholic-religious than most of Europe. Jacket and tie for the opera, but even there you won't be thrown out. Just embarrassed.

Language

The Viennese speak German but with many local *Wienerisch* colloquialisms that incorporate Yiddish, Hungarian and Czech words (their 19th-century empire once incorporated these countries, and many more). Always start

Good Reading
- **Bachmann**, **Ingeborg**, *Songs in Flight*. Bilingual edition of poems.
- **Clare**, **George**, *Last Waltz in Vienna*. The destruction of a family 1842–1942.
- **Gainham**, **Sarah**, *Night Falls on the City*. Jewish wartime Vienna.
- **Gay**, **Peter**, *Mozart*. Easy-to-read Mozart biography.
- **Greene**, **Graham**, *The Third Man*. Bombed Vienna and black market intrigue.
- **Hamann**, **Brigitte**, *Hitler's Vienna*. Where the dictator picked up most of his violent prejudices.
- **Höpler**, **Vogel et al**, *Vienna City Guide for Children*.
- **Jelinek**, **Elfriede**, *The Piano Teacher*. The novelist was awarded the 2004 Nobel Prize for Literature.
- **Kerr**, **Philip**, *A German Requiem*. Spooks in postwar Vienna.
- **Roth**, **Joseph**, *Radetzky March*. Nineteenth-century Vienna.
- **Zweig**, **Stefan**, *The Burning Secret and Other Stories*. Delicious tales of *fin-de-siècle* Vienna.
- **Rubenfeld**, **Jed**, *The Interpretation of Murder*. A novel.
- **Silva**, **Daniel**, *A death in Vienna*. A thriller.

with *Grüss Gott* ('God's greetings') wherever you are and with everybody. Except perhaps in some taxis, suburbs and the countryside, everyone seems to speak English.

Toilets

The 300-plus public toilets in Vienna are marked WC. Not all are open 24/7. Keep a 50 cent coin on you. Toilets are much rarer in the suburbs. U-Bahn stations usually have toilets. Most cafés will allow you to use their toilet even if you're not a guest.

Special Interest Groups

Tips for the Disabled: The Austrian Tourist Board has a leaflet 'Vienna for Visitors with Disabilities', ⌨ www.austria.info The Vienna Tourist Office Albertinaplatz/ Maysedergasse, ☎ (01) 24 555, is ⌚ open daily 09:00–19:00. It has booklets, e.g., on

hotels for the disabled plus a disabled booking service. Some sidewalks – but not all public transport – are at street level. Some buses have fold-out ramps. The old historic trams are not good for the disabled. Guiding stripes on the Underground indicate the exit, elevator and escalator options for folk in wheelchairs. Wiener Linien, ☎ (01) 7909-0, have U-Bahn and rail station maps in Braille. There's a database (⌨ www. you-too.net) that will give you a good idea about the accessibility of public places in Vienna. Being an old city, quite a few of Vienna's many attractions are in historic buildings that are not always access-friendly. There are special guided tours; try ⌨ www.info.wien.at

Student Travellers

There are nine youth hostels in Vienna. You will need an International Youth Hostel

Federation member's card which you can get at the hostels. In the high season, 1 July to 30 September, the hostels tend to revert to being busy hotels. Try the Austrian Youth Hostel Association, ✉ Schottenring 28, ☎ (01) 533 5353. If you are an EU citizen you can work in Vienna, so if your German is good, give it a go. The Club International Universitaire (CIU), 🖳 www.ciu.at and ☎ (01) 533 6533, gives advice to foreign students. Apart from the University of Vienna's inexpensive 9- and 12-week German-language courses (🖳 www.univie.ac.at/wihok) there are at least five other language institutions giving intensive German courses (2–3 weeks).

Gay and Lesbian Travellers

The Regenbogenparade (Rainbow Parade) takes place in Vienna on the last Saturday in June, 🖳 www.pride.at The Naschmarkt likes to think of itself as home to the gay district. There are some 8 gay and lesbian nightspots and the Rosa–Lila Villa flies the rainbow flag. Frauen Café is strictly for women; ✉ 8, Langegasse, II 🚇 U2 Lerchenfelderstrasse, Josefstadt). If the Viennese have hang-ups about sexuality, they don't let on.

Women Travellers

No special problems. Half the City Council are women. Men may be macho up in the mountains, but they have learned to be good boys in Vienna.

Senior Travellers

Women over 60 and men over 65 can sometimes get cheaper tickets on all Vienna's transport. Try the Senioren-Service, ☎ 4000 8580, for options available, plus leisure and cultural activities.

INDEX OF SIGHTS

General Index

Page numbers given in **bold** type indicate photographs

General Index

Limerick
County Library